25 BICYCLE TOURS IN VERMONT

Coasting past the Kreffer covered bridge near West Arlington.

25 BICYCLE TOURS IN VERMONT

A Revised and Expanded Edition of 20 Bicycle Tours in Vermont

John S. Freidin

Photographs by the Author

Backcountry Publications   Woodstock, Vermont

For my parents   Doris and Jesse Freidin
that we might have ridden these roads together

An Invitation to the Reader—Although it is unlikely that the roads you cycle on these tours will change much with time, some road signs, landmarks, and other items may. If you find that changes have occurred on these routes, please let us know so we may correct them in future editions. The author and publisher also welcome other comments and suggestions. Address all correspondence:

Editor, *Bicycle Tours*
Backcountry Publications
PO Box 175
Woodstock, VT 05091

Library of Congress Cataloging in Publication Data

Freidin, John S.
   25 bicycle tours in Vermont.

   Rev. ed. of: 20 bicycle tours in Vermont. c1979.
   1. Bicycle touring—Vermont—Guide-books.
2. Vermont—Description and travel—1981   —Guide-
books. I. Freidin, John S. 20 bicycle tours in Vermont.
II. Title. III. Title: Twenty-five bicycle tours in
Vermont.
GV1045.5.V5F73   1984   917. 43'0443   84-70168
ISBN 0-942440-18-8

©1979, 1984 by John S. Freidin
Published by Backcountry Publications
Woodstock, VT 05091
Printed in the United States of America
Photographs by the author
Design by Dick Widhu

Acknowledgements for the First Edition

The tours are the joint products of all the men and women who have led trips, fixed bicycles, and written letters for Vermont Bicycle Touring; I shall always be in their debt. But special thanks go to Marge Dethloff, Sally Dorsey, and Bruz Brown. For the sake of this book they relieved me of many responsibilities; for the sake of our friendships they ignored my short temper and preoccupation. And without the enthusiastic support of the people who have ridden with Vermont Bicycle Touring, I would have lacked both the incentive and leisure to write. This is their book too.

My research was made immeasurably easier by the previous work of others, but errors of fact and judgment remain fully mine. I relied especially heavily on three books: Ray Bearse, ed., *Vermont: A Guide to the Green Mountain State* (3rd edition, 1968), grandchild of the Federal Writers' Project guide sponsored by the Works Progress Administration of the New Deal; William Hancock *et al.*, eds., *The Vermont Atlas and Gazetteer* (1978); and Madeleine Kunin and Marilyn Stout, *The Big Green Book: A Four-Season Guide to Vermont* (1976). Finally, for her patience as well as her insight I am grateful to editor Catherine Baker.

Acknowledgements for the New Edition

First, I want to thank all those cyclists who were out riding and using the first edition when I met them. The pleasures of those many encounters have added a precious extra dimension to the satisfactions of writing this book. I look forward to meeting many more readers in the future.

In revising the original twenty tours and developing the five new ones, I have been very fortunate to have had the insightful assistance of my colleague Deborah Young. Preparation of the finished manuscript was made easy for me by the cheerful and wonderfully competent help of Cindy Fuller, with whom I also work. These two women deserve special thanks, but everyone at Vermont Bicycle Touring has helped.

In addition to the publications I relied upon for the first edition, I was able this time to benefit from the knowledge and research of Christina Tree and Peter Jennison, thanks to their book, *Vermont: An Explorer's Guide* (The Countryman Press, 1983). Finally, it has been a pleasure working with editors Chris Lloyd and Sarah Spiers at Backcountry Publications. They have made this a better book.

Bristol, Vermont
14 December 1983

foreword

When I think of bicycle touring, I think of Vermont. When I think of organized bicycle tours, I think of John Freidin. When I'm asked what is the standard of excellence for organized tours, I recommend John's outfit, Vermont Bicycle Touring.

That said, it is my pleasure to write a foreword for the new and revised version of his popular *20 Bicycle Tours in Vermont*—now 25— as he's added five tours. Bicycle touring, with a group, or alone, is a particular pleasure because it combines pleasure and fitness in an appealing package. But if you're not prepared for a tour, or the tour has not been scouted and road tested by experienced cyclists, your joy on the road might not be long-lasting.

Why I can recommend this book so highly is that I've worked with John for years and know he *knows* a great deal about selecting and road-testing tours. You can be assured that these tours, in terms of the diversity and beauty they offer, take you to the heart of Vermont. Moreover, in selecting the tours John has been careful to provide tours which can be modified in hundreds of ways to meet your particular cycling and recreational needs. In effect, you have hundreds of touring options in this book.

As an experienced cyclist, John has made sure that these tours take you to places that will add miles of pleasure to your recreational cycling. If you want to shop, swim or rest during your tour, this book will show you how. Perhaps most important, *25 Bicycle Tours in Vermont* presents the essence of bicycle touring: traveling under your own power to beautiful places at a pace that suits you. That is the ultimate in independence.

And the formula will be found in this book.

James C. McCullagh
Editor & Publisher
Bicycling *Magazine*

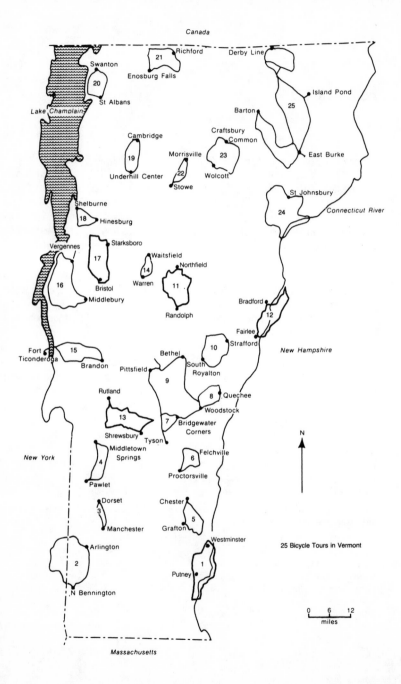

Canada

Richford
21
Enosburg Falls
Swanton
20
St Albans

Lake Champlain

Derby Line
Island Pond
25
Barton
East Burke

Cambridge
19
Underhill Center
Morrisville
22
Stowe
23
Wolcott
Craftsbury
Common

St Johnsbury
24
Connecticut River

Shelburne
18
Hinesburg

Starksboro
Vergennes
17
Bristol
Middlebury

Waitsfield
14
Warren
Northfield
11
Randolph

Bradford
12
Fairlee
Strafford

Fort
Ticonderoga
15
Brandon

Bethel
10
Pittsfield
9
South
Royalton

New Hampshire

Rutland
13
Shrewsbury
Tyson
7
8
Quechee
Woodstock
Bridgewater
Corners

New York

Middletown
Springs
4
Pawlet
6
Felchville
Proctorsville

Dorset
3
Manchester
Chester
5
Grafton

N

Arlington
2
N Bennington
Westminster
1
Putney

25 Bicycle Tours in Vermont

0   6   12
miles

Massachusetts

Contents

Introduction

Caterpillars and butterflies. On a ride one day, it struck me that bicyclists could be either one. The difference is their views of the terrain. To caterpillars every hill looks like a mountain, while to butterflies even mountains look level as they float over them. But given time every caterpillar grows into a butterfly. To me this is the greatest beauty of bicycling: that everyone in good health can become a proficient rider simply by doing it. Thanks to the efficiency of bicycles, most cycling requires only a little strength and no agility or speed.

This book is for both caterpillars and butterflies. Whether you have not ridden in years or cycle a thousand miles a season, *25 Bicycle Tours in Vermont* will guide you to routes matching your ability in one of the most exquisite cycling environments imaginable. It will enable you to find your way with confidence; it will alert you to hills and hazards; it will suggest places to swim, find food, and get your bicycle repaired; and it will deepen your enjoyment of what you see by telling you a little about the history, architecture, geology, wildlife, and other curiosities along the way.

I have selected the following twenty-five tours for their beauty and diversity. Each one had to be beautiful; and, as a group, they had to provide a breadth of choices wide enough to suit every level of cyclist and unveil as many facets of Vermont life as possible. In length they range from 16 to 155 miles; in terrain from flat to very hilly. Some tours can be fully enjoyed on a three- or five-speed bicycle; most are best ridden on at least a ten-speed. The tours are dispersed throughout the state from North Bennington to Derby Line, from Lake Champlain to the Connecticut River. But every tour ends where it begins. There are overnight tours and day trips, trips to country inns and trips to campgrounds, trips laden with history and trips through remote wonderlands, trips that visit handsome villages and trips that take you swimming, fishing, and bird-watching.

The nine hundred and fifty miles covered by these tours all stem from trips run by Vermont Bicycle Touring. By leading those trips since 1972, I have ridden all the roads many times and learned how thousands of other cyclists, from novices to experts, have felt about them. Their reactions have guided my appraisals of the terrain; their misadventures have helped me compose directions that at last, I hope, are clear to all.

Many places are beautiful, but beauty alone does not satisfy the needs of bicyclists. Vermont is a cyclist's delight not merely because of its beauty, but because of its scale and temperament. Here, where we live in villages not cities, worship in churches not cathedrals, and travel on roads not highways, the environment is scaled to human proportions. Seldom do more than ten miles separate general stores; rarely does a climb remain arduous for more than two miles. The pace of Vermont life more closely resembles the speed of a bicycle than that of an automobile; and the friendliness of the people is more like the cooperation of tandeming than the competitiveness of motoring. To bicycle is to steep yourself in an environment; to do so in Vermont is to fall in love with both the place and the pedaling.

Selecting a Tour

From the state map on page 8, see which tours fall in an area you find interesting or convenient. To facilitate your locating them on the map and in the text, the tours are grouped into four regions, roughly equal in size. Next, look up the tours you are considering to see which suit you in terms of distance and terrain. Then read their introductions, which describe their principal features, and make your choice.

The twenty-five tours really present far more than twenty-five choices. A tour is not the same ridden in one season as it is ridden in another; ridden with friends as ridden alone; ridden in the rain as ridden in the sunshine; ridden when leaves are on the trees as ridden when the trees are bare. And once you know a ride well in one direction, do it in the other and you will discover a new tour.

For each tour the round-trip distance and the difficulty of the terrain are stated at the beginning of the tour description. The terrain is rated according to the length, steepness, and frequency of the hills you must climb. If you want to know more precisely the nature of the terrain, read the entire tour. There I have tried to describe every hill that is either very steep or lasts at least a mile. But remember, since every tour completes a circle, every inch of climbing is matched by an inch of descent. Furthermore, no two bicyclists make the same assessment of every hill or even find the same hill equally difficult every time they ride it. Here are what my ratings mean:

Easy terrain is generally level and never produces more than one and a half miles of uphill riding for every twenty-five miles of touring. Easy terrain is well suited to three- and five-speed bicycling.

Easy-to-moderate terrain is also generally level but requires one and a half to three miles of climbing for every twenty-five ridden and brings some fast downhill runs. This terrain also suits three- and five-speed bicycling, though a ten-speed will make it easier.

Moderate terrain necessitates three to six miles of ascent for each twenty-five miles of riding and is best ridden on at least a ten-speed bicycle with a low gear in the mid-forties or less.*

Moderate-to-difficult terrain requires climbing three to six miles for roughly every fifteen miles of touring, and the grades are likely to be steeper than on moderate terrain. Gearing reaching into the thirties is helpful.

Difficult terrain also requires three to six miles of climbing for each fifteen miles of riding, but the hills are often steep. Gearing in the low or mid-thirties is desirable.

Vermont terrain is never really level, and consequently bicycling here is more challenging than in most other places. If you want to be cautious, just assume that I have slightly underestimated the difficulty of the tours. But don't be timid.

I have seen thousands of people, many with no recent bicycling experience or special conditioning, comfortably ride up to thirty miles over easy or easy-to-moderate terrain. Although the effort tired many of them, very few had real difficulty. In age they ranged from seven to seventy.

Preparing for a Tour

Numerous materials have been written on conditioning, equipment, eating, camping, and packing for bicycle tours. I deal with these topics only in a very limited way. If you want thorough guidance, consult Bikecentennial or one of the other sources in the Appendix.

The best way to get in shape for bicycling is to bicycle. Other sports, such as swimming or running, help, but they do not place identical demands on your body. To build your stamina, bicycle frequently and regularly—at least two or three times a week—and gradually increase the distance and speed you ride.

Several days before starting a tour carefully read the entire tour description. Decide what to carry with you—such as food and bathing suit—and what to get along the way.

The tours are described in a regular pattern. Beside each of the cumulative mileages are the directions to follow to stay on the route. The mileages are given to help you gauge the times between turns, not to suggest that you use an odometer, though one can be helpful. Most touring cyclists average seven to twelve miles an hour. Advice about

---

*To determine the lowest gear on your bicycle count the teeth on the smaller front chain ring, divide that number by the number of teeth on the largest cog of the freewheel, and then multiply the quotient by the diameter, in inches, of the rear wheel.

terrain, road surface, or places to buy food is stated in one of the paragraphs following the directions that take you there. Similarly, historical, architectural, and other curious information about an area follows the directions that take you there.

Make sure your bicycle is in good repair. Bicycles need over-hauling at least every two thousand miles or two years. Careful atten-tion should be paid to brakes, drive train, shifting apparatus, wheels, headset, tires, and the tightness of the seatpost, saddle, and handle-bars. Vermont has many bicycle shops, but they are often some dis-tance from these tours. A list of the closest shops is given at the end of each tour. Before going, call ahead to make certain you can get the parts and expertise you need. Whenever you tour, carry at least a pump and equipment for repairing flat tires.

Saddle soreness is common to cyclists. Within limits you grow accustomed to your perch, and proper cycling pants also help. But the saddle itself makes a major difference, especially for women, since nearly all saddles are designed to fit men. Most touring cyclists, myself included, prefer a broken-in leather saddle or one of the orthopedi-cally designed models such as those made by Avocet. Avocet has developed a woman's saddle that is highly praised by virtually every woman I know who uses it.

"A Vermont year is nine months winter and three months damn poor sleddin'." At least according to proverb. Although there are won-derful days for cycling in April and November, the principal bicycling season here runs from May through October. I like May and June best, because the days are long and the landscape is brilliantly green and strewn with wildflowers. July and August are rarely too hot or humid to be uncomfortable and offer great swimming. The fall foliage season, covering roughly four weeks from mid-September to mid-October, turns the trees into a riot of color, but the likelihood of cold or wet days is greater. Vermont weather is extremely volatile. From May through August daytime temperatures can range from 40° to 90° F. (4° to 33° C.). During September and October they can go from 30° to 80° F. (−1° to 27° C.). Prepare yourself for a variety of temperatures even within a single day by dressing in layers.

Select clothing that breathes as well as insulates. Your muscles should be kept warm, especially your legs and knees, and your skin should be kept dry except on the hottest days. Wool accommodates the widest range of temperatures, dries quickly, and warms you even when it gets wet. On cool days you can increase your comfort by wearing a lightweight polypropylene undershirt beneath a wool jer-sey. Polypropylene does not retain water and helps wick perspiration away from your skin.

On bright days use clothing and lotion to protect yourself from sunburn. A visor keeps the sun off your face and the rain off your

Across the Missisquoi River to Jay Peak.

glasses. To prevent irritation, your pants should have neither seams nor folds that you must sit on. Gloves, especially ones with padded palms, help prevent your hands from numbing and offer some protection if you fall. Better protection comes from cautious cycling and a hard helmet, such as those made by Bailen and Bell. Your shoes should be tied with double knots to prevent a lace from catching in the chain and have soles adequate to prevent the pedals from hurting your feet. Raingear poses a problem, because most materials that keep the rain out lock the sweat in. In light rains I am most comfortable in one or two wool jerseys. For cold or heavy rain a well-ventilated jacket made of a breathable fabric like Gore-Tex is best. And all your outer clothing ought to be brightly colored—preferably yellow, orange, or red—to make you highly visible.

You should carry water, preferably in a bottle mounted on your bicycle, and a little food. Drink before you are thirsty and eat before you are hungry to keep your strength and spirits up. Good food for snacks include bananas, oranges, granola, nuts, and raisins. You need little protein but lots of fluid and carbohydrates. Consider carrying a camera and film; books about birds, wildflowers, or trees; a first-aid kit; a bathing suit; a towel; a pocket knife; and money. Each tour description is accompanied by a sketch map, but an official Vermont state road map would also be helpful (see Appendix).

For day trips you can readily pack what you need in a handlebar bag or a bag that hangs from your saddle. For overnight tours add panniers, which attach to the rear carrier and hang on either side of the rear wheel. In selecting panniers, insist on ones that mount firmly so they cannot swing into the spokes of your wheels.

Doing a Tour

Read the full tour before you start. Then, when you are riding, pause at each turn to read the directions for the next turn, for it may come within a tenth of a mile. All the roads on all the tours are paved unless the directions state that they are not. If you find yourself on an unpaved road not mentioned in the directions, you have gone off course. The text also describes the most prominent grades. If nothing is stated about terrain, the road is relatively level.

Even more than hills, wind can affect cyclists, for the wind can be your escort, friendly or antagonistic, all day long. Be aware of the wind by watching tall grass and leaves. By recognizing a headwind you can factor that obstacle into the rating of the tour and avoid taking on more than you want. And by recognizing a tailwind you can avoid inflating your ability to the point where you attempt more than you can enjoy.

In order to use the proper muscles, your legs must extend almost fully when the ball of your foot is on the center of the pedal—as it should be when you are cycling—and the pedal is at its lowest point, six o'clock. In that position your leg should bend only slightly at the knee. If it bends more than that, you will tire quickly and be more susceptible to cramps. An easy way to determine the correct height for your saddle is to sit on it, place your heel on a pedal, and then push the pedal to six o'clock. You then should be able to extend your leg fully without having to lock your knee. Make sure whenever you adjust your saddle that you leave at least two inches of seatpost inside the frame.

A ten-speed bicycle is not made to be pedaled as a three-speed. The larger number of gears is designed to conserve your energy by enabling you to keep your legs turning at a relatively constant speed regardless of terrain, wind, or road surface. Once you get the knack, you will find it far less tiring to maintain an even cadence than to change your rate of pedaling, as you must on a three-speed. Further-more, it is easier to spin your legs quicky, pushing proportionately less strenuously each time, than to turn them slowly and push harder. If you are a beginner, try to maintain a cadence of fifty to seventy revolutions of each foot a minute. As you master that rate, gradually increase your cadence to about eighty-five, which is excellent for touring. (Bicycle racers spin ninety to one hundred twenty revolutions a minute.)

Cycling on unpaved roads requires special attention and care. Bicyclists using very lightweight one-inch or 25 mm wired-on tires or tubular tires* may have some difficulty handling their bicycles on these roads. Furthermore, using lightweight, and therefore narrow cross-section, tires on unpaved roads increases the likelihood of punctures. When a narrow tire hits a stone hard enough, the tire is compressed so much that the tube gets pinched against the rim of the wheel and can be cut. To minimize the chance of punctures, keep your tires fully inflated to the pressure indicated on the tire and wipe them free of debris. It is best to use tires that accommodate at least ninety pounds, because they are more resistant to puncture than low-pres-sure tires and also produce less rolling resistance.

Vermont law stipulates that "every person riding a bicycle is grant-ed all of the rights and is subject to all of the duties applicable to operators of vehicles, except . . . those provisions which by their very

---

*Tubular tires, also called sew-ups, are used mostly by bicycle racers, who prefer them because they are lighter and take more air pressure—hence producing less rolling resistance—than conventional, wired-on tires, of-ten called clinchers. Circular in cross section, tubulars fully enclose their tubes by being sewn together on the inside face. They fasten to the rims of bicycle wheels with glue or two-faced sticky tape. Made of extremely light materials, tubulars are more delicate than wired-ons. The relative advan-tages of tubulars have been greatly reduced by the recent development of lightweight, high-pressure clinchers.

nature can have no application." It also says that cyclists "shall ride as near to the right side of the roadway as practicable," to which I would add a warning not to ride so close to the edge of the pavement that you risk going off it by looking at something other than the road. Several regulations govern bicycling after dark, which it is best not to do at all. Violations of these or other Vermont bicycle laws are punishable by fine.

To these laws I would add seven more: (1) Use a bicycle flag, for it makes you more quickly visible to motorists; (2) If you wear corrective lenses to drive a motor vehicle, wear them when you bicycle, for you must see at least as well; (3) Ride single file, keeping several bicycle-lengths between you and the cyclist in front of you—and more going downhill—so you do not risk running into one another; (4) Never turn to look behind you while you are operating a bicycle unless you have proven in an open parking lot that you can turn around without permitting your bicycle to alter its course; (5) Never bicycle across railroad tracks, for the slipperiness of the rails plus the spaces between the rails and the road are very likely to cause your bicycle to slip from under you and spill you off; (6) MOST IMPORTANT—NEVER make a left turn while you are riding. Stop, get off your bicycle, look, and then walk across, please; (7) Always wear a hard bicycling helmet.

Very few cyclists can conquer every hill. But before walking, try a trick I learned from two Maryland grandmothers. When you reach your lowest gear and can no longer turn the pedals, stop and stand by your bicycle for one minute but no longer. Such pauses, known as "granny stops" by cyclists who have ridden with Vermont Bicycle Touring, relieve your pain and allow your body to gather enough energy to resume pedalling. You can climb nearly any hill more quickly and easily by taking "granny stops" than by pushing your bicycle.

Some dogs like to chase bicycles. Fortunately in Vermont most dogs are tied up and will reach the end of their tethers long before they reach you. However, if a dog does give chase, remember never to change your course in order to escape, for the dangers of going off the road or into the traffic greatly exceed those posed by the dog. If the dog is very menacing, get off your bicycle, use it as a shield between yourself and the animal, and walk out of its turf.

Finally, it is to your advantage not to stop to rest until you have ridden long enough to warm up. That usually takes forty-five minutes to an hour. When you do stop, limit your rest to fifteen minutes, for a longer pause cools you so much that you have to begin warming up all over again. This suggestion is emphatically not intended to discourage your stopping to investigate things that interest you or to talk with people along the way. After all, that is what bicycle touring is all about.

Southern Vermont

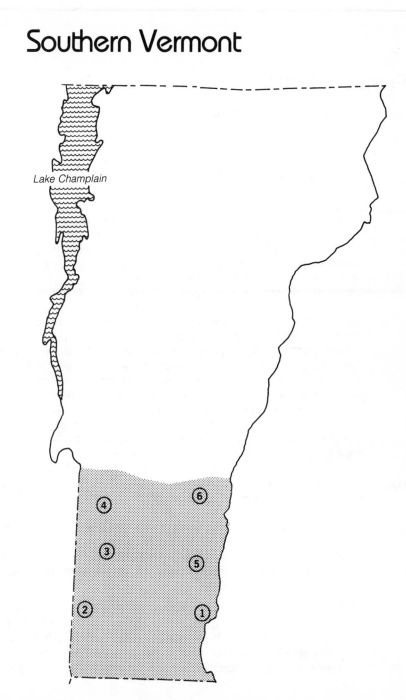

Lake Champlain

1

Putney–Westminster

Moderate terrain; 41.5 or 37 miles

The Putney region abounds with activity and beauty. The tour focuses on the splendidly rural Connecticut River valley and offers an interesting diversity of water scenes, farmland, orchards, and dense woods. The terrain is moderate, but there are plenty of hills, and, though most are short, they are unusually steep.

For years Putney has attracted skilled weavers, blacksmiths, cabinet makers, and other craftspeople. Many have studios in or near the village. Carol Brown Woolens and Green Mountain Spinnery, both known for fine natural fiber fabrics, are located in Putney. So is the Putney Nursery, which grows the largest selection of wildflowers in the eastern U.S. On the first weekend in October, oarsmen and women from far and wide convene here for a major rowing regatta.

This tour owes much to my special friends, Betsy Bates and Neil Quinn; Betsy has been leading tours for Vermont Bicycle Touring since 1976, and she and Neil run one of Vermont's finest bicycle/ski shops. So it's appropriate to start the tour at their West Hill Shop, which has a large parking area as well as a superlative staff. The West Hill Shop, which is open seven days a week, sits at the end of a long driveway that opens onto Depot Road just opposite the Putney Inn, an eighth-mile east of Exit 4 off Interstate 91.

0.0 Turn LEFT out of the driveway of the West Hill Shop onto Depot Road, which is unsigned here, and ride uphill toward US 5 and Putney Village.

Just before you turn onto Depot Road, you are facing the Putney Inn and a local information booth. The inn has comfortable motel-style rooms and a pleasant bar and dining room. Consider stopping at the information booth to get the latest news about local events.

The communes that flourished in Putney and elsewhere throughout Vermont during the 1960s and early 70s had forebears in Putney 130 years earlier. As Ralph Waldo Emerson commented at that time: "The ancient manners were giving way. There grew a certain tenderness on the people, not before

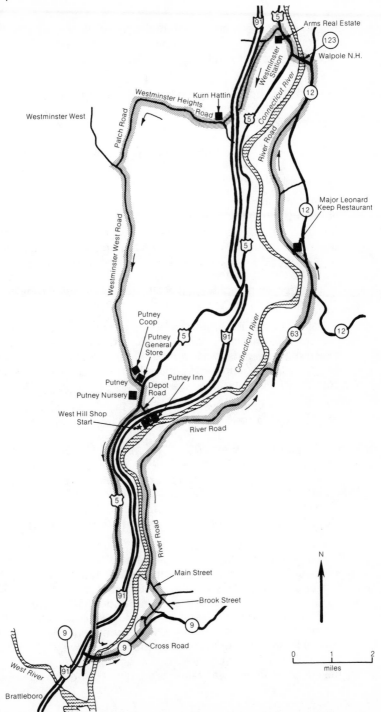

Arms Real Estate

Walpole N.H.

Westminster Station

Westminster Heights Road

Kurn Hattin

Westminster West

Patch Road

Connecticut River

River Road

Major Leonard Keep Restaurant

Westminster West Road

Putney Coop

Putney General Store

Putney

Putney Nursery

Putney Inn

Depot Road

West Hill Shop Start

Connecticut River

River Road

River Road

Main Street

Brook Street

Cross Road

West River

Brattleboro

N

0   1   2
miles

remarked. It seemed a war between intellect and affection.
...The key to the period appeared to be that the mind had
become aware of itself."

A hundred thirty years ago in Putney, John Humphrey Noyes,
the son of an upstanding family and a graduate of Yale, decided
that humankind was no longer corrupted by original sin.
Instead, like the children of the Sixties, Noyes believed all
persons might achieve perfection on earth and so created a
community to sustain his beliefs. His followers practiced Bible
Communism: the sharing of all labor and property. "All mine
thine, and all thine mine."

What distinguishes Noyes from other Christian socialists of his
time and connects his community so closely with those of the
Sixties is his view of sexual freedom. Noyes saw little distinction
between owning property and owning persons. "The same spirit
which abolished exclusiveness in regard to money, would
abolish...exclusiveness in regard to women and children."
Noyes' community practiced Multiple Marriage, whereby adults
shared sexual intimacy and child care alike.

Eventually, even Putney could no longer tolerate Noyes' radical
views, so he and his followers fled to Oneida, New York, where
their religious and social concerns were transmuted into the
aesthetic and commercial concerns of the famous silver plate
company they founded.

Noyes' experiment clearly presaged the communes of recent
times. Looking back on his father's Putney community, one of
Noyes' sons recalled a quality of life strikingly similar to the
communal life of the 1960s: "The relation between our grown
folks had a quality intimate and personal, a quality that made life
romantic. Unquestionably the sexual relations of the members
under the Community inspired a lively interest in each other, but
I believe that the opportunity for romantic friendships also
played a part in rendering life more colorful than elsewhere."

0.2   At the top of the hill, turn LEFT onto US 5 South.
Contemporary Putney is rightfully known for apples (a tenth of
Vermont's crop), athletes (Olympians Bill Koch, Tim Caldwell,
and Eric Evans), artists (Jim Dine), authors (John Irving and John
Caldwell), and of course Aiken—the Honorable George—gover-
nor, senator, and horticulturalist. Best known of all is the Putney
School (1935), an innovative private coeducational boarding
school for 200 students, grades nine through twelve. Life at the
Putney School carefully integrates academic study with work on
the school and its small farm. "We harvest our own vegetables,

sing Bach together, and live close to the land and weather."

Before turning south on US 5, you might want to pick up some food in Putney. To reach the village turn right onto US 5 North and ride a quarter-mile. The Putney Coop makes fine fresh sandwiches, and the Putney General Store next door has a delightful soda fountain and wide selection of groceries.

As you head down US 5, the road rolls over a few short hills.

6.9   At the Traffic Light, turn LEFT onto Route 9 East toward Keene.
       In a third-mile, you cross the Connecticut River and enter New
       Hampshire. The Connecticut rises at the conjunction of the Ver-
       mont, New Hampshire, and Canadian borders and flows 412
       miles southward into Long Island Sound at Old Saybrook. It is
       New England's longest river and separates Vermont and New
       Hampshire for the 235 miles of their common border.

       In the early spring (April through mid-May), thousands
       of waterfowl migrate up the river. Take a little time and you may
       sight Canada goose, snow goose, black duck, wood duck, scoter,
       horned grebe, ringnecked duck, merganser, herring gull, and
       common goldeneye.

       There are thirteen dams along the Vermont/New Hampshire sec-
       tion of the river. Most are owned by New England Power Company
       and generate electricity during times of high demand. As a result
       the water level changes as much as twelve feet at places.

       After you cross the river, which is the lowest point on the tour, you
       climb uphill for a half-mile.

9.0   Turn LEFT onto Cross Road, which is the first paved road you reach on
       the left.
       Be careful of traffic on Route 9 as you turn.

9.4   At the Stop Sign at the crossroad, go STRAIGHT to continue on Cross
       Road.
       In a quarter-mile, Cross Road dives down a winding, steep hill.
       Ride cautiously.

9.8   At the Stop Sign, turn LEFT onto Brook Street, which is unsigned.

9.9   The next Stop Sign, bear LEFT onto Main Street which becomes River
       Road.

10.3   At the intersection, go STRAIGHT to continue on River Road.
       During the next seven miles you ride up and down several short
       steep hills, some as long as three-quarters of a mile.

18.3   At the Yield Sign, turn LEFT onto New Hampshire Route 63 North.
       Thereafter, stay on Route 63, which is the main road; do not turn onto
       the side roads.
       Route 63 rolls over two half-mile hills.

20.5   At the Stop Sign, go STRAIGHT onto New Hampshire Route 12
       North.
       Beware of the traffic at this intersection.

21.1   Just before you pass Major Leonard Keep Restaurant on the left, turn

LEFT off Route 12 onto the unsigned road that goes downhill.
Cross Route 12 very cautiously. In a mile the road is so broken up that for about forty yards it seems as though there is no pavement at all.

As you approach the next intersection, you will be riding down a hill and around a curve that bends to your right. Be sure to go very slowly, for the road is often littered with sand and gravel.

23.0 Turn LEFT onto River Road.

25.4 At the Stop Sign, turn LEFT onto New Hampshire Route 12 North.

26.8 At the second blinker, turn LEFT onto New Hampshire Route 123 toward Westminster, Vermont, and ride back across the Connecticut River.

27.2 At the T in Westminster Station, turn RIGHT toward US 5 and Interstate 91 and ride 25 yards up a short hill to the Stop Sign. There, bear slightly RIGHT onto US 5 North.
If you want to reduce the tour by four and a half miles and follow terrain that is a bit less hilly, just turn LEFT onto US 5 South and let it lead you back to Depot Road in Putney.

In 1775 Westminster witnessed one of the first outbreaks of violence between the New York colonial authorities and the people living in the area we now know as Vermont. The Yorkers claimed jurisdiction over all land between Lake Champlain and the Connecticut River. So did New Hampshire. And neither would honor land grants made by the other. In order to preserve their rights to land granted them by both authorities, Vermonters convened in Westminster on January 16, 1777, and declared their independence of both New York and New Hampshire. This step soon led to Vermont's separate nationhood and refusal to join the original thirteen colonies when they formed the United States. Not until 1791 did Vermont agree to become the fourteenth state. Vermont's first newspaper, *The Green Mountain Post Boy*, began publication here in 1781.

27.9 Beside Arms Real Estate on the left, turn LEFT toward Interstate 91.
If you reach Allen Brothers Farm Store on the left, you have ridden 150 yards beyond your turn. But if you're hungry stop at the Farm; it offers a tempting selection of fresh fruit and other snacks.

28.4 At the first left (just before the exit off Interstate 91), turn LEFT onto Westminster Heights Road toward Kurn Hattin and Westminster West. After about five miles this road is called Patch Road.

In two and four-tenths miles you reach the boys' campus of Kurn Hattin, a private, non-profit residential school for grades one through eight. Kurn Hattin, named after a hill in Israel, specializes in helping boys—and girls on a campus in Saxtons River—from disturbed homes.

Follow the main road straight through the campus; do not turn onto the sideroads. From Kurn Hattin you head up a tough three-mile hill that gets steeper as you approach the top. The climb is immediately followed by a steep descent for about a mile, a short climb, and then another steep, and also winding, descent that carries you to your next turn.

35.0 At the intersection near Westminster West, turn sharply LEFT onto Westminster West Road toward Putney.
After a relatively easy mile, you reach a sharp three-quarter-mile "wall", but thereafter it's largely a downhill run all the way back to Putney.

40.8 At the Stop Sign in Putney, bear RIGHT onto US 5 South.

41.3 Just beyond the Putney Nursery on the right, turn LEFT onto Depot Road toward the Public Boat Landing and Interstate 91.

41.5 Turn RIGHT into the entrance to the West Hill Shop, where this tour began.

Bicycle Repair Services
Andy's Cycle Shop, 536 West Street, Keene, NH (603-352-3410)
Bicycle Barn, 56 Main Street, Northfield, MA (413-498-2996)
Bicycle World, 104 Federal Street, Greenfield, MA (413-774-3701)
Norm's Ski & Bike Shop, Junction of Routes 12 and 101, Keene, NH (603-352-1404)
Red Circle, Inc., 143 Main Street, Brattleboro, VT (802-254-4933)
Specialized Sports, Putney Road, Brattleboro, VT (802-352-1404)
Toy City, 114 Main Street, Keene, NH (603-352-3131)
West Hill Shop, Depot Road, Putney, VT (802-387-5718)

2

Arlington–North Bennington

Moderate terrain; 46.5 miles

Southwestern Vermont and adjacent New York are Norman Rockwell Country. This tour, more than any other in the book because it follows unpaved roads one-third of the way, is especially fun to ride on a mountain or all-terrain bike. But it does not require such a bicycle; I've enjoyed it many times on a regular ten-speed. By using unpaved roads, the tour neatly avoids the region's busy highways. Virtually traffic-free, these unpaved backroads connect you more intimately with the natural surroundings than do most paved roads. Following wooded lanes and lush valleys between ridges of the Green and Taconic mountains, the route offers several fine views. If you have the time and a fishing license, you can try your luck in some of the greatest trout water in the country, because for ten miles you cycle along the famous Batten Kill. Or you can swim in that river beneath a red covered bridge by the house where Norman Rockwell lived. The tour also takes you past a reconstructed eighteenth-century country tavern and a hundred-year-old Victorian mansion, both now museums and open to the public. You start in Arlington.

0.0   From the intersection of Routes 7A and 313 in Arlington follow Route 7A South two hundred yards and then turn LEFT onto East Arlington Road toward East Arlington.

Just before you turn, you pass the Norman Rockwell Gallery on the left. Located in an old white church, the gallery exhibits many of Rockwell's *Saturday Evening Post* covers. Admission is free. Rockwell lived in West Arlington from 1939 to 1953 and did most of his illustrations of small town American life while he was here.

Arlington was also home of Dorothy Canfield Fisher, the immensely popular chronicler of Vermont life.

Connecticut Anglicans settled Arlington in 1763 so they might enjoy the amenities permitted by their faith in a more tolerant climate than puritanical Connecticut. Under their influence Arlington became the first Vermont town to take such liberties as raising maypoles and decorating Christmas trees.

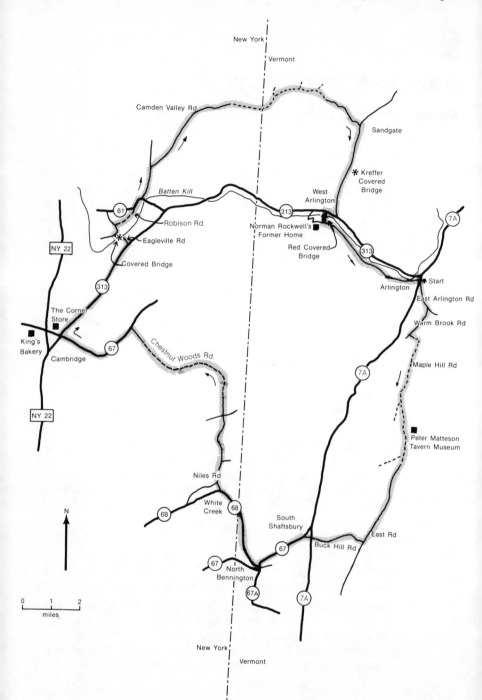

The St. James Cemetery, in Arlington, bears witness to the early presence of these Episcopalians. One of Vermont's oldest burial grounds, it contains many curious headstones. Called Tory Hollow during Revolutionary times, Arlington was a Loyalist stronghold but also briefly the residence of Ethan Allen, whose two children and first wife, Mary Brownson, are buried in St. James Cemetery.

Since there are no other places to buy food for twelve miles, you may want to stop at the Arlington Country Store or Cullinan's Store, which faces East Arlington Road on the left one hundred yards after you cross Route 7A.

0.8   Turn RIGHT onto Warm Brook Road.

1.8   Turn LEFT onto Maple Hill Road. (At its southern end in South Shaftsbury, this road is called East Road.)
In two-tenths of a mile Maple Hill Road becomes unpaved for five miles. The first three are well packed and shaded; the balance may be soft and have loose rocks on its surface. After a level quarter-mile, Maple Hill Road goes gently but steadily uphill for a mile and a quarter and then flattens out for a mile and a half.

4.8   At the fork bear LEFT to stay on Maple Hill Road, which is still unpaved.
The next mile is the most demanding, for the road ascends more steeply than before, and its surface gets soft.

As the slope of the hill tapers off, you reach the Peter Matteson Tavern Museum (on the left). Records from 1784 indicate that this building served as a public house as well as the homestead of a two-hundred-acre farm. Although fire destroyed most of the original structure in 1976, it has been rebuilt and furnished with early American antiques. The staff, which maintains the museum and works the farm in an eighteenth-century manner, is especially hospitable to people who arrive by bicycle. The museum is open between noon and 4:00 p.m. on Fridays, Saturdays, Sundays, and holiday Mondays from mid-May to mid-October and by appointment (802-442-5225). Admission is charged.

Beyond the museum, the road climbs gently for slightly under a mile and then becomes paved and level.

9.6   At the first paved road on the right, turn RIGHT onto Buck Hill Road. (There is probably no road sign at this corner.)
Buck Hill Road runs rapidly downhill to South Shaftsbury, dropping from a height of 1,200' to 740' in less than two miles.

11.5   At the traffic light in South Shaftsbury, go STRAIGHT across Route 7A onto Church Street, the sign for which is on the right on the far side of Route 7A.

11.9   Just after crossing the railroad tracks, bear LEFT onto Route 67 West, called Eagle Street here.

13.9   At the intersection beside the Merchant's Bank (on the right) in North Bennington, turn RIGHT to continue on Route 67 West, called Bank Street here.

   If you follow the signs for the Park-McCullough Mansion from the bank to the corner of West and Park streets, you can visit that elegant Victorian residence. Built in 1865, the thirty-five room mansion exemplifies the extravagant tastes and life style of midnineteenth-century tycoons. It is well worth the time to see its grand stairway, opulent rooms, bizarre furniture, marble mantels, parquet floors, Persian rugs, outdoor sculptures, and collections or carriages and Victorian clothing. Tours of the mansion begin between 10:00 a.m. and 4:00 p.m., Sundays through Fridays from mid-May through October. Admission is charged.

14.1   At the fork, bear RIGHT off Route 67 onto the road toward White Creek, New York. (In New York this road is called County Road 68.)

   In a mile and a quarter, you cross the state line into New York.

17.7   At the sweeping left curve, go STRAIGHT off County Road 68 onto Niles Road toward Cambridge and Eagle Bridge.

18.0   At the fork, bear RIGHT to continue on Niles Road.

18.4   At the crossroad, go STRAIGHT onto Chestnut Woods Road, which at its end in five miles is called Chestnut Hill Road.

   For three of the next four and a half miles, the road is unpaved. The paved portions, which come in several small pieces, are in very poor shape and may actually be less pleasant for bicycling than the unpaved parts. In a half mile you begin climbing for one and a half miles. The first half is very steep; the second half is gradual.

23.0   At the Stop Sign, turn LEFT onto Route 67 West.

25.1   At the Stop Sign in Cambridge, New York, turn RIGHT onto Route 313 East.

   The Corner Store, directly in front of you at this Stop Sign, treats bicyclists generously and makes good fresh sandwiches. If you ride past The Corner Store so that the front steps are on your right and continue straight across Route 22 a half-mile into the center of Cambridge, you will find King's Bakery on your left.

Their confections are a treat.

30.1 Turn LEFT off Route 313 onto Eagleville Road.

30.7 After going through the covered bridge, turn RIGHT onto the unsigned road.

31.1 At the first paved road on the right, turn RIGHT onto Robison Road, which in one-tenth mile becomes unpaved.

31.9 Bear RIGHT onto County Road 61, which is paved. (There is probably no route marker at this turn.)

32.3 At the corner where County Road 61 turns right to cross the Batten Kill, go STRAIGHT onto the unsigned road.

33.1 At the fork beside a white house with a stone retaining wall in front (on the left), bear RIGHT onto Camden Valley Road. Follow the signs for Sandgate and Camden Valley Road for the next eight miles.

In three and a quarter miles the pavement ends. Camden Valley Road is then unpaved but well packed for two and a half miles, which slope gently uphill. A quarter-mile after the surface becomes paved again, the road shoots sharply downhill through a series of tight S-curves usually littered with loose gravel. These conditions last three-quarters of a mile and must be ridden cautiously. After the curves, the road continues moderately downhill for one and a quarter miles more.

41.0 At the T in Sandgate, which is merely an intersection, turn RIGHT toward West Arlington onto Sandgate Road, though there may not be a street sign there.

For the next three miles you descend gently, almost without pause, back to the Batten Kill. About halfway down you pass the Kreffer covered bridge on your left. In 1977 designer Susan De-Peyster and carpenter William Skidmore converted an open-planked bridge spanning the Green River here into this short covered bridge.

43.1 At the Stop Sign in West Arlington, which is little more than this intersection, turn RIGHT onto Route 313 West, which may be unsigned at this corner.

43.4 At the red covered bridge on the left, turn LEFT onto the unsigned and unpaved road that goes through the bridge.

The bridge, built in 1852, stretches 80 feet across the Batten Kill. The swimming here is excellent and can be reached most easily from the shore at the far end of the bridge.

43.8 At the T, turn LEFT onto River Road, which is unpaved.

As you approach this T, the house to your right is the one where

Norman Rockwell lived for fourteen years. It is now a private residence and not open to visitors.

45.0 At the first bridge, turn RIGHT onto the unpaved and unsigned road.

47.0 At the next bridge turn LEFT onto the unsigned road. You will then ride across the Batten Kill.

If you go two-tenths of a mile uphill away from the river to the West Mountain Inn, you can treat yourself to a fine dinner and excellent selection of wines and beers. This inn is a favorite stop on Vermont Bicycle Touring trips, and innkeepers Wes and Mary Ann Carlson are superb hosts.

47.1   At the Stop Sign, turn RIGHT onto Battenkill Drive, which is also Route 313 East.

46.5   At the Stop Sign, you are back in Arlington at the intersection of Routes 313 and 7A, where you began.

Bicycle Repair Services
Battenkill Sports, Routes 11 and 30, Manchester Center, VT (802-362-2734)
Giard's Bike Shop, 208 North Street, Bennington, VT (802-442-3444)
Up and Downhill, Inc., 160 Ben Mont Avenue, Bennington, VT (802-442-8664)

3

Dorset–Manchester

Easy terrain; 25 miles

For over a century genteel colonial and Victorian residences have made Dorset and Manchester summer, and more recently winter, retreats for cosmopolitan Easterners. Following shaded backroads past magnificent homes and then skirting open fields at the bases of Mount Equinox (el. 3,816′) and Mother Myrick Mountain (el. 3,290′), this route also leads to many distinctive shops, eateries, and cultural attractions, such as the Southern Vermont Art Center and the Dorset Playhouse. Well-groomed farms of horse and cattle breeders nestle beneath the mountains aligning the valley where you bicycle along the Batten Kill. Marvelous swimming awaits you at the old marble quarry in Dorset. The tour begins and ends by the village green in Dorset.

0.0   Leave Dorset on Church Street, which runs west from Route 30 between the village green and the Dorset Inn (1796), Vermont's oldest continuously operated inn. If you are looking for food, you can buy a freshly made sandwich and choose from a wide selection of other items at Peltier's General Store, directly across the green from the Dorset Inn.

Originally a center of trade and finance for local farmers, Dorset has grown over the last hundred years into a community of wealthy seasonal residents, retired persons, and other exurbanites. They have meticulously preserved the town's architecture and brought it a cultural vitality that supports a summer theater, a dance program, and several antique and craft galleries. The United Church of Dorset and East Rupert (1912), on your left as you leave town, is built of Dorset marble and decorated with stained glass windows that depict local pastoral scenes. The Dorset Playhouse can be found on Cheney Road a block south of the church.

1.0   At the Stop Sign, turn LEFT onto West Road.

In a mile and a half at the corner of West and Nichols Hill roads you pass on your right a state historical plaque marking the site of the Cephas Kent Tavern. There in 1776 Ethan Allen's Green Mountain Boys proclaimed Vermont's independence of New

Hampshire and New York. From 1777 until 1791, when it became the fourteenth state, Vermont was an independent nation.

5.0   At the Stop Sign, turn RIGHT onto Route 30 South.

5.6   Just beyond the Mobil station (on the right), turn RIGHT onto Manchester West Road.

Within a half-mile, you begin climbing the only hill on this tour. It rises gradually for a mile and three-quarters. After the plateau at the top, you ride downhill nearly two miles to Manchester. Halfway down on your right is the entrance to the Southern Vermont Art Center, which offers concerts as well as exhibitions

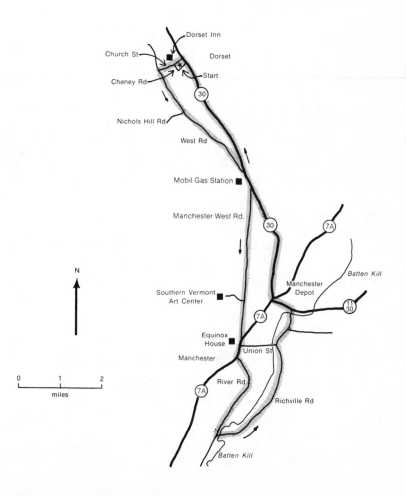

of the work of local artists. Its Garden Cafe serves lunch from 11:30 a.m. to 3:00 p.m. and reservations are advised. For reservations and information about concerts and exhibitions, call (802-362-1405). From the first weekend in June until mid-October, the center is open from 10:00 a.m. to 5:00 p.m., Tuesdays through Saturdays, noon to 5:00 p.m. on Sundays, and 10:00 a.m. to 5:00 p.m. on those Mondays that are holidays. Admission is charged.

9.3   At the Stop Sign in Manchester, go STRAIGHT onto Route 7A (Main Street) South.

Immediately on your right, beside the Johnny Appleseed Book-shop, and behind a sidewalk of marble slabs, stands the white, columned Equinox House. This formerly elegant hotel, provided its Victorian guests with stables and horse carriage service to and from the railroad station in Manchester Depot.

From here it is only a mile—straight south on Route 7A—to Hildene, the grand Georgian Revival mansion, built for Robert Todd Lincoln in 1904. This 24-room monument to turn-of-the-century wealth and exclusiveness has been carefully restored and authentically furnished. It is now open to the public. Tours include a brief demonstration of the 1,000 pipe organ which can be played manually or with one of the 240 player rolls. Hildene is open from 9:30 a.m. to 4:30 p.m., daily, mid-May through October. Admission is charged to see the house but not to visit the grounds, which make a delightful place to picnic and walk.

9.6   Just beyond the sign on your left for the Ekwanok Country Club, turn LEFT onto River Road.

River Road begins with a fast, curving descent that grows gentle after a half-mile and lasts two miles.

12.1   Beside a bridge (on the left) and a white farmhouse (on the right), turn LEFT toward Manchester Depot onto Richville Road, the first possible left turn off River Road.

You immediately cross a bridge over the Batten Kill, one of Vermont's most prolific wild trout streams.

16.6   At the tiny traffic island, bear LEFT to stay on Richville Road.

17.1   At the Stop Sign in Manchester Depot, turn LEFT onto Route 30 North (also Route 11 West and Depot Street).

18.0   At the traffic light, turn RIGHT to stay on Route 30 North, which at this point is also US 7.

Along US 7, within a mile north and south of this intersection you can find most of Manchester's galleries, shops, and eating places. This stretch of highway is not well suited for bicycling, because it is heavily traveled and narrow. Should you wish to browse in the village, leave your bicycle locked and walk.

18.2   At the traffic light, turn LEFT to stay on Route 30 North.
When riding on Route 30, beware of high-speed traffic and leave enough space between every three cyclists for a milk truck to pass and pull safely in front of you. These large trucks do not have sufficient braking ability to slow down or stop quickly.

In about four and a half miles opposite a one-story white building, a path on the right side of Route 30 leads to the Dorset quarry, at its opening in 1758 the first commercial marble quarry in America. Dorset marble has been used for public buildings not only in Vermont but throughout the country. However, for years no mining has taken place here, and the quarry, now filled with spring water, makes a beautiful swimming hole. Actually there are two quarries—one within twenty yards of the road and

Robert Todd Lincoln's Hildene (1904) in Manchester.

a second, popular with skinny-dippers, about a hundred yards beyond the first. Both are open to the public for unsupervised swimming.

25.0 When you reach the Dorset Inn (on the left), you are back where the tour began.

Bicycle Repair Services
Battenkill Sports, Routes 11 and 30, Manchester Center, VT (802-362-2734)

Green Mountain Schwinn Cyclery, 133 Strongs Avenue, Rutland, VT (802-775-0869)

Sports Peddler, 158 North Main Street (US 7), Rutland, VT (802-775-0101)

4

Pawlet–Middletown Springs

Difficult terrain; 30 miles

Following very quiet roads through pastoral countryside, this tour begins in Pawlet and visits the small Victorian resort of Middletown Springs. The healing powers of the iron and sulphur springs in Middletown drew nineteenth-century ladies and gentlemen to "take the waters" nearly a century ago. Although the springs have not been in commercial use for a long while, the springhouse beside a fern-lined brook was recently rebuilt and makes a delightful resting place. Rolling farmlands stretch from the road's edge to sugar-bushes on the foothills of the surrounding Taconic and Green mountains. There are a few long views of these two mountain ranges, but generally the setting is intimate rather than grand.

0.0   Leave the intersection in Pawlet by heading north on Route 133 toward Middletown Springs.

Set at the convergence of Flower Brook and the Mettawee River, Pawlet prospered as a mill town a hundred and fifty years ago. At the falls in the center of this tiny village stands a handsome, though idle, waterwheel, twenty-seven feet in diameter and four feet wide. Johnny Mach built the wheel during the depression of the 1930s to supply his general store and home with electricity.

1.0   At the fork, turn LEFT to stay on Route 133 North, toward Middletown Springs.

Within a mile you begin climbing a two-mile hill. From the top the road descends for one and a half miles and then rolls the rest of the way to Middletown Springs. As you enter the village of Middletown Springs, a small unpaved road leads off the right side of Route 133 to Mineral Springs Park and the restored springhouse. The stream is too shallow for swimming but makes a delightful place to cool off and refill your water bottle. You can buy a snack either at the general store on the right just before the turn-off for the park or at Grant's Store opposite the village green.

11.0   At the Stop Sign in Middletown Springs, turn RIGHT to stay on Route 133 North, which at this intersection merges with Route 140 East.

Over the next five miles, you ride mostly uphill as you ascend nearly 400′ to Tinmouth at 1263′.

13.0 At the intersection, bear RIGHT onto Route 140 East toward Tinmouth.

16.0 At Tinmouth, just beyond Tully's Place (on the left), go STRAIGHT off Route 140 onto the unsigned road that leads to Danby Four Corners. As soon as you leave Route 140, you pass on your left the garage of the Tinmouth Volunteer Fire Department. For the next seven miles, follow the signs for Danby and Pawlet.

Tinmouth served as a small iron manufacturing center with its own furnace and forges from the 1780s until 1837, when they were abandoned. Now small farms and a few summer homes

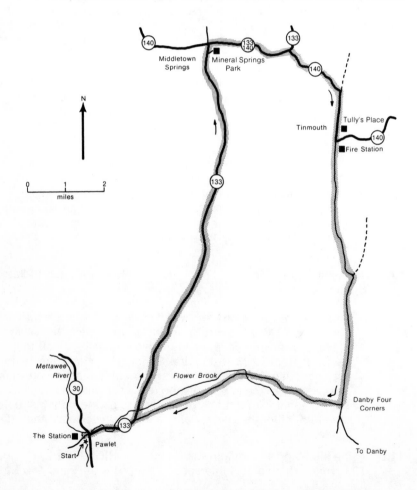

dominate the town. Tully's Place, which serves pleasant, simple food, is a good spot to eat.

23.0 At the intersection in Danby Four Corners, turn RIGHT onto another unsigned road which is the first paved road on your right since Tinmouth. After you make your turn, you will pass the front of the Mountain View Baptist Church on your left. Look carefully for this turn to avoid riding to Danby, which lies four miles downhill off the route.

Just beyond Danby Four Corners you begin the final climb of the tour. You must pedal uphill for about one and a half miles, but then you begin a long beautiful descent that extends nearly without interruption all the way to Pawlet.

29.0 At the Stop Sign, go STRAIGHT onto Route 133 South toward Pawlet.

30.0 At the Stop Sign, you're back in Pawlet where you began.

The Station Restaurant in Pawlet.

Flower Brook offers excellent swimming just upstream of Johnny Mach's old waterwheel. It is easiest to reach the water from the north side of the river by the post office. Seventy-five yards down a side road west of Route 30 The Station Restaurant, built in an old train station and decorated with railroading memorabilia, serves ice cream and sandwiches.

The Pawlet Potter, Marion Waldo McChesney, has her studio across the street from The Station. Her gracious manner makes visiting her shop a real treat. Ask to see her butter dishes and spongeware.

Bicycle Repair Services

Battenkill Sports, Routes 11 and 30, Manchester Center, VT (802-362-2734)

Green Mountain Schwinn Cyclery, 133 Strongs Avenue, Rutland, VT (802-775-0869)

Sports Peddler, 158 North Main Street (US 7), Rutland, VT (802-775-0101)

4/27/87

Blue; Sunny; Cool; Well traveled Rt. 103 w/ a wide

5

Chester—Grafton
shoulder; nice vistas; shaky road conditions; Stonehearth
Easy-to-moderate terrain; 26.5 miles
Inn- very pretty + rustic. Overall, beautiful ride.

Starting by the long, slender green that splits the main street of Chester, this tour passes some of Vermont's most beautiful early architecture. Following the broad shoulder of the Calvin Coolidge Memorial Highway southeast through the Williams River valley, the route comes to an interesting eighteenth-century burial ground and provides delightful views of rocky pastures and rolling hills. It then turns south onto a small road through woods of sugar maples only occasionally interrupted by the clearing of a small farm. Changing direction again outside the village of Saxtons River, the tour continues west on a narrow, winding old stagecoach road that draws you into the scenes it passes as if no road existed at all. Then, after a pause in the jewellike town of Grafton, you head back to the stone house village of Chester, where you may complete the day with a fine dinner at the Chester Inn.

0.0 From the Chester green follow Route 11 (Main Street) East.

In the early part of the nineteenth century a family of masons by the name of Clark settled in Chester and turned its talents to building stone houses. Constructed of locally quarried gray-green mica schist, these gracious, unpretentious homes make Chester a special place. Often a full two and a half stories high, many contain secret rooms where before the Civil War blacks seeking freedom from slavery hid as they fled northward on the underground railway. Most of the stone houses face Route 103, both north and south of its intersection with Route 11.

If you like maps, do not miss the National Survey Company, headquartered in Chester. The Survey's excellent maps are sold and displayed in its office on Main Street. Chester has several groceries, although you need not carry much food since you can shop or eat at restaurants in Saxtons River and Grafton.

0.7 At the intersection, continue STRAIGHT off Route 11 onto Route 103 South, the Calvin Coolidge Memorial Highway.

As you cycle down the wide shoulder of Route 103, you are following a route developed by Indians as a footpath and used by the colonists as a bridle path and military road. In 1849 the Rutland Railroad Company laid tracks over that path to link Rutland with Boston, thereby creating a new market for Vermont dairy products.

7.0   Turn RIGHT onto Pleasant Valley Road toward Saxtons River. The signs for both are on the left side of Route 103.

Instead of turning toward Saxtons River, you may enjoy venturing off the route to see the Rockingham Meeting House (1787). It sits on a knoll on your right one and a half miles south of here just off Route 103. This two-story clapboard structure is one of the best examples of Federal-style church architecture in New England. Inside are a high pulpit and box pews, each accommodating 10 to

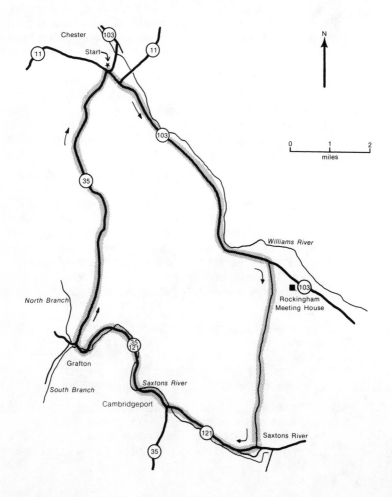

15 people, some of whom must sit facing away from the pulpit. Around back lies the old cemetery, which contains some of the most interesting gravestone carvings in Vermont. The carvings are delicately etched on fragile, weathered slate, so if you make rubbings treat the stones very gently.

12.0 At the Stop Sign on the outskirts of Saxtons River, turn sharply RIGHT onto Route 121 West.

Route 121 is narrow and winding. On the curves ride carefully close to the edge of the pavement, because the bends in the road often prevent motorists from seeing you until they are practically on top of you. Here you are following an old stagecoach road along the Saxtons River, a challenging white-water run in early spring.

If you would like a delicious lunch served in a cheery, handsome setting, turn left instead of right at this stop sign and ride a half-mile to the Saxtons River Inn. In 1903 this building was built as an inn but then served as a private home for many years before being imaginatively reconverted to an inn in 1974. It is on the left side of Main Street as you enter town. Call ahead (802-869-2110) to make sure the dining room is open.

Before leaving Saxtons River you might enjoy looking at the old country kitchen and excellent early photographs maintained by the Saxtons River Historical Society and displayed on the ground floor of West Church. The collection is open from July 1 to September 15 on Saturdays, Sundays, and holidays between 2:30 p.m. and 5:00 p.m. There are also two antique shops and a general store on Main Street.

15.0 At the T in Cambridgeport, turn RIGHT to continue toward Grafton on Route 121 West, which here joins Route 35 North.

19.0 At Grafton, turn RIGHT onto Route 35 North toward Chester.

The story of Grafton bears telling, because it is unique. Surrounded by low-lying hills at the confluence of the Saxtons River's two branches, Grafton has ridden the crests of prosperity and the troughs of depression. In the 1820s nearly fifteen hundred people lived there and thrived on the profits of thirteen soapstone quarries and many water-powered mills, including two which loomed the fleece of some ten thousand sheep pastured on the surrounding hillsides. As Grafton flourished, its people built themselves not only churches and private homes of fine design and workmanship, but a magnificent inn, now called the Old Tavern. With this facility Grafton became a town of distinction, hosting over the years such prominent guests as Henry Thoreau, Ulysses Grant,

Theodore Roosevelt, Woodrow Wilson, and Rudyard Kipling.

But near the end of the century decline set in. Sheep farmers moved west in search of fresh grazing land, and woolen mills moved south in search of cheap labor. One by one the industries that had produced Grafton's wealth disappeared. By the end of the Great Depression fewer than four hundred persons called Grafton home, and nearly all eighty houses in the village were up for sale at rock bottom prices.

Then, in 1963, thanks to the great foresight and generosity of Pauline Dean Fiske and her nephews, Matthew Hall and Dean Mathey, the Windham Foundation was born. Its purpose is the town's resuscitation; its means, the purchase of real estate and the restoration of buildings. Over the past fifteen years the Foundation has brought and rehabilitated more than twenty buildings, including the Old Tavern, the Village Store, a dairy farm, a blacksmith's shop and several private houses, many of which are now leased to their former owners. To bolster the town's economy, the Foundation created the Grafton Village Cheese Company, and to protect open lands, it acquired over a thousand acres around the village. That land is maintained for wildlife conservation, hiking, and cross-country skiing. This massive, continuing effort has brought Grafton out of a long sleep into a new, but very different, life. Though many jobs have been created, the success of the Foundation has pushed the price of real estate beyond the reach of many former residents, and once again turned the Old Tavern into a gracious and friendly inn, but one which few can afford. Newcomers have moved in, and many oldtimers have left.

Still, Grafton is not a museum-town. It is a lively place where people live and work and govern themselves by town meeting. Most of the buildings are not open to the public because they are privately occupied. But much of interest is visible from the outside, and several buildings can be visited. Information and maps are available at the front desk of the Old Tavern. Along the side streets you can find several art galleries and antique shops, a museum, and two covered bridges. The Village Store extends a warm welcome to bicyclists and sells fine sandwiches as well as a good selection of fresh fruit, wines, Grafton cheese, and fudge.

Immediately upon leaving Grafton on Route 35 North, you climb a steep but short hill. After a half-mile the slope tapers off to a moderate grade lasting a mile and a half. Then, after passing through woods, the road turns a corner and descends quickly two and a half miles into Chester.

26.3 At the Stop Sign, turn LEFT onto Route 11 West.

26.5 You are at the Chester green, where you began the tour.

Bicycle Repair Services
A. B. Carpenter, Route 103 (North Street), Chester Depot, VT (802-875-2676)
Bixby's Bicycle Shop, Route 103, Ludlow, VT (802-228-3532)
The Cyclery Plus, US 4, West Woodstock, VT (802-457-3377)
Red Circle, Inc., 143 Main Street, Brattleboro, VT (802-254-4933)
West Hill Shop, Depot Street, Putney, VT (802-387-5718)

6

Proctorsville–Felchville

Moderate terrain; 26 miles

Starting in the old mill town of Proctorsville, this tour carves a circle through hardwood forests and quiet farmlands. No important towns, museums, or historical sites border the route; its attraction lies in the beauty of the countryside around you. Bicycling nearly the entire way within sight of rivers or streams, you twice have good places to swim. The tour's only difficult stretch—three and a half miles uphill along a sometimes rough, unpaved road—comes near the beginning and is amply rewarded by delightful views of a peaceful valley and the charm of a road shaded by a canopy of trees. Otherwise the terrain is easy and includes a six-mile descent. If you are seeking a genuinely pastoral ride, this tour is hard to beat.

0.0 From Gilcris' Store in the center of the tiny village of Proctorsville, follow Route 131 East.

0.3 Turn LEFT off Route 131 onto Twenty Mile Stream Road.
A half-mile outside Proctorsville, Twenty Mile Stream Road ascends steeply for a half-mile and then gradually for three miles more. The next three and a half miles, which are unpaved, climb steadily up a grade that remains moderate until the last mile, which is steep. Although the road surface is well-packed, loose rocks and washboardlike bumps may slow you down.

Three-quarters of a mile from Proctorsville watch the left side of the Twenty Mile Stream Road for a sign resembling a football with two diagonal stripes in the middle. It marks the entrance to the Proctorsville Potter and Weaver, where Alan and Wendy Regier keep shop from 10:00 a.m. to 6:00 p.m., daily except Tuesday.

7.0 At the T, turn RIGHT onto Kingdom Road, which is the first paved road you reach after Twenty Mile Stream Road becomes unpaved. (No road sign is posted at this turn.)
For three-quarters of a mile, Kingdom Road goes uphill. Then it turns sharply downhill and carries you swiftly down one of Vermont's most exhilarating descents. If you maintain a slow speed, you can pick your own swimming hole in the North

Branch of the Black River. Along your way you can also see Mt. Ascutney (el. 3,144') on your right.

13.7   At the Stop Sign in Felchville (Reading P.O.), turn RIGHT onto Route 106 South.

Before leaving Felchville, if you are the least bit hungry, go into the Reading Country Store, on your left when you reach this Stop Sign. It has been catering to the needs of bicyclists for many years and during that time cheered up more than one cold and wet rider. The store makes incredibly generous sandwiches to your specifications and has a good selection of wines, fresh fruit, and other groceries. You can picnic on the lawn of the town hall across the street from the store or by the Black River.

The Reading Historical Society Museum beside the town library on Route 106 contains old furniture, clothing, paintings, photographs, and an unusual collection of advertising cards and old music. The museum is open by appointment only. Call Howard Sanderson at 802-484-5005.

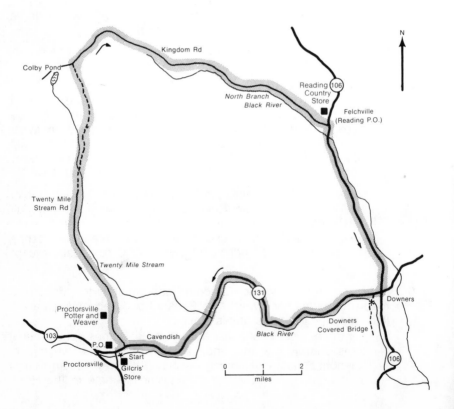

17.8 At the blinker in Downers, turn RIGHT onto Route 131 West.
In three-tenths of a mile, look carefully to your left for a small unpaved road leading diagonally off Route 131. If you follow that road two hundred yards, you will find the Downers covered bridge, built around 1840. Below it lies a shallow, pleasant swimming hole in the Black River.

Six miles west of Downers, just after you have ridden up a short rise that is the only significant incline on Route 131, you come into the small town of Cavendish. Cavendish has several marvelous gingerbread houses and an old stone meetinghouse as well as two small general stores, all of which face Route 131. Cavendish's most famous resident is Alexander Solzhenitsyn.

26.0 You are back in Proctorsville, where this tour began.

Bicycle Repair Services
Bixby's Bicycle Shop, Route 103, Ludlow, VT (802-228-3532)
Green Mountain Schwinn Cyclery, 133 Strongs Avenue, Rutland, VT (802-
  775-0869)
Sports Peddler, 158 North Main Street (US 7), Rutland, VT (802-775-0101)
The Cyclery Plus, US 4, West Woodstock, VT (802-457-3377)

Central Vermont

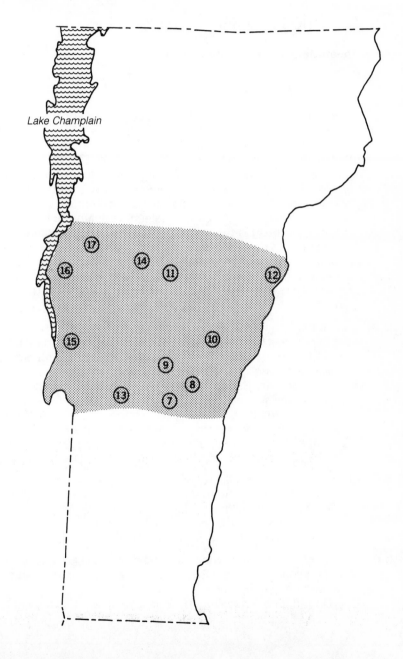

Lake Champlain

7

Tyson–Bridgewater Corners

Easy–to–moderate terrain; 29 or 19 miles

This tour will please anyone fond of lakes or American history. From Tyson you follow the Black and Ottauquechee rivers and the shorelines of Echo, Amherst, and Woodward lakes. A visit to Plymouth, the tiny hill town where Calvin Coolidge was born, provides a nostalgic and informative look at American country life fifty to a hundred years ago. The Vermont Division of Historic Sites carefully maintains the Coolidge home, the Vermont Farmers Museum, and several other early nineteenth-century buildings in Plymouth. By starting in Tyson, the tour passes Echo and Amherst lakes twice and puts at the trail's head the fine facilities of Echo Lake Inn: a dining room, lounge, swimming pool, tennis court, and lakeside dock with canoes and rowboats. Cyclists who prefer a nineteen- rather than twenty-nine-mile tour can begin in Plymouth Union at the junction of Routes 100 and 100A (mileage 5.0 below).

0.0 Leave the Echo Lake Inn in Tyson by riding north on Route 100.
For the first two miles the road follows the curved shores of Echo and Amherst lakes. The latter takes its name from Lord Jeffrey Amherst who in 1759 directed the construction of the Crown Point Military Road. The road, which Route 100 traces through this valley, was cut out of the wilderness from Charlestown, New Hampshire, to Lake Champlain. In the winter of 1775 Colonel Henry Knox and his army of farmers used the road to haul fifty-nine cannons overland from Fort Ticonderoga to Boston where they played a critical role in driving out the British.

5.0 Turn RIGHT onto Route 100A North toward Plymouth.
Immediately the road curves up what many bicyclists call Hysteria Hill. Although barely a half-mile long, it is heart-pounding steep. However, once you reach the top, Route 100A takes you delightfully downhill for nearly six miles.

6.0 Four-tenths of a mile beyond the crest of Hysteria Hill and just past a pond on your right, turn LEFT onto the road to Plymouth and ride a quarter-mile to that village.
On Independence Day, 1872, in a weathered cottage attached

to the general store in Plymouth, the thirtieth president of the United States, Calvin Coolidge, was born. (Only one other Vermonter, Chester A. Arthur, has occupied the presidency.) After completing secondary school at Black River Academy in nearby Ludlow, Coolidge attended Amherst College and embarked on a legal and political career in Massachusetts. Inaugurated governor in 1919, he quickly drew national attention by calling out the National Guard to supress a Boston police strike. Only a year later, he was elected vice-president as Warren G. Harding's running mate. Then, at three in the morning of August 3, 1923, while vacationing at his family home in Plymouth, Coolidge was awakened with the news of Harding's

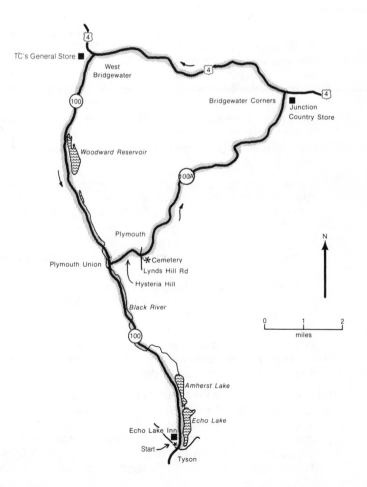

death. The vice-president's father, a notary public, swore his son into office as president.

Coolidge completed Harding's term and won election in his own right in 1924. The taciturn, penurious Vermonter—whose campaign slogan was "Keep Cool with Coolidge"—may seem an ironic figure to have been president at the height of the Roaring Twenties. But he loyally gave big business a free rein, and the booming economy and wild speculation in the stock market bouyed his popularity. Indeed he might well have been re-elected had he chosen to run again. Coolidge is buried at Plymouth beside his wife and son in a simple grave adorned only with his name and the presidential seal.

Plymouth deserves a leisurely visit. The Coolidge homestead and the cottage where the president was born have been meticulously preserved. Their furnishings and architecture present an accurate glimpse of life in Vermont at the turn of the century. Nearby, in a mammoth old barn, the Vermont Farmers Museum displays an instructive and beautiful collection of antique farm implements. These tools show how tasks now done by electricity and fossil fuels were once accomplished by human and animal power. From late May until mid-October, these buildings are open between 9:30 a.m. and 5:30 p.m. daily. Admission is charged.

Across from the Coolidge home stands the Union Christian Church (1840). Its exterior resembles those of many other clapboard churches in Vermont. But its interior was ingeniously rebuilt in 1890 out of rare, local hard pine in a style known as carpenter Gothic, because it achieves with wood the Gothic forms normally constructed from stone. The new Calvin Coolidge Memorial Center displays late nineteenth- and early twentieth-century photographs, mostly related to the life of Calvin Coolidge and captioned with quotations from his autobiography. At the north end of the village, the Plymouth Cheese Corporation merits a visit, especially on weekdays when you can see its unique curd cheese being made. The village also contains a small restaurant at Wilder House, picnic tables, and two shops that sell local crafts.

6.5   Retrace your way from Plymouth to the Stop Sign at Route 100A and turn LEFT onto Route 100A North toward Woodstock.

The village cemetery where Coolidge is buried sits a quarter-mile from this intersection on a pretty knoll overlooking the surrounding hills. To get to the cemetery, go straight across Route 100A onto Lynds Hill Road. After your visit retrace your way back to Route 100A and turn right onto it. Route 100A follows Broad Brook gently downhill for nearly six miles.

12.5 At the Stop Sign in Bridgewater Corners, turn LEFT onto US 4 West.

The Junction Country Store, at the corner of this intersection, sells fresh sandwiches as well as a fine selection of food, drink, and country merchandise. Bicyclists are always welcomed.

US 4 is more heavily traveled than other roads on this tour, but it offers a wide paved shoulder most of the way. Though it may not look that way, you will be riding slightly uphill for the next six miles as you follow the Ottauquechee River upstream. I have seen a great blue heron and other interesting birds here.

18.7 At the blinker in West Bridgewater, turn LEFT onto Route 100 South
and follow it to your starting point (either five miles to Plymouth
Union or ten to Tyson).

On your right immediately after turning onto Route 100 stands
TC's General Store, which makes good fresh sandwiches.
Directly behind the store, The Back Behind Saloon, dimly lit and
decorated with antiques, serves good lunches and dinners.

The first two miles of Route 100 go gradually uphill to the
northern end of Woodward Reservoir.

23.8 You are at Plymouth Union by the junction of Routes 100 and
100A.

29.0 The Echo Lake Inn in Tyson is on your right.

Bicycle Repair Services

Bixby's Bicycle Shop, Route 103, Ludlow, VT (802-228-3532)
Green Mountain Schwinn Cyclery, 133 Strongs Avenue, Rutland, VT (802-
775-0869)
Sports Peddler, 158 North Main Street (US 7), Rutland, VT (802-775-0101)
The Cyclery Plus, US 4, West Woodstock, VT (802-457-3377)

8

Woodstock–Quechee

Moderate terrain; 24.5 miles

This tour combines village elegance and rural tranquility. It starts in Woodstock, where Vermont's most stately architecture has been meticulously preserved. Although the village often bustles with traffic and pedestrians by late morning, the route neatly avoids that commotion by following rarely used roads through the quiet countryside north of town. With the exceptions of two difficult climbs, the tour is not demanding and features one of Vermont's finest downhill runs, nearly seven miles long. Slightly over two miles at the tour's end are not paved, but they suit two-wheel travel well.

0.0 From the Woodstock green follow Route 12 (Elm Street) North toward Barnard.

Before leaving, take at least a quick tour along the backroads of this town. Vermont's most distinguished nineteenth-century townhouses line Woodstock's oval green and shaded side streets. Since 1786 the shire town of Windsor County, Woodstock has always managed to be a center of wealth and gracious living and always avoided being a place for manufacturing. Finance and commerce, not industry, have kept this town both prosperous and beautiful. Perhaps its former wealthy residents shielded Woodstock from change; certainly its most recent residents have tried. Telephone and electrical wires are buried; signs are kept to a minimum; and in 1969, when a new bridge was needed to cross the Ottauquechee River, the town built a covered bridge in authentic Town Lattice style, using only wooden pegs to hold it together.

Despite a year-round stream of visitors, Woodstock has little of the garishness that plagues many popular towns. Reserved, urbane, and exclusive, Woodstock's appeal derives from the pristine charm of its homes and the tastefulness of its expensive shops. Four churches—the First Congregational (1807), St. James Episcopal (1907), the Universalist (1835), and the Masonic Temple, formerly Christian Church (1827)—still ring bells cast by Paul Revere.

The Woodstock Historical Society, housed in the 1807 home of neurologist Charles L. Dana, exhibits a superior collection of early nineteenth-century antiques, including locally made furniture, portraits, silver, farm implements, quilts, doll houses, and etchings by John Taylor Arms. Behind the house an exquisitely landscaped garden stretches to the Ottauquechee River. The Society is located at 26 Elm Street and open from Memorial Day through October, Monday through Saturday, 11:00 a.m. to 5:00 p.m., and Sunday, 2:00 p.m. to 5:00 p.m. Admission is charged.

During the warm weather the town hosts many special events, including an antique automobile rally, a major AKC dog show, and several craft exhibits on the green. There is far more to see than can be mentioned here. Fortunately the Woodstock Chamber of Commerce publishes an annotated map of the village. You can get one free from the Information Booth on the green or

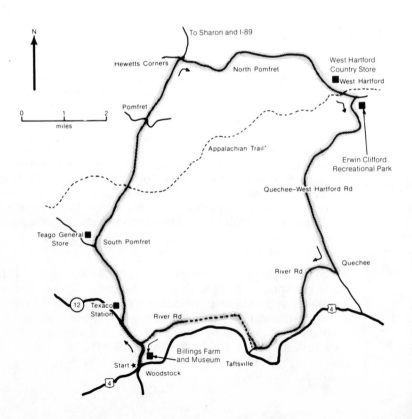

at the Chamber's office at 4 Central Street. Before leaving town, you might also want to pick up some food, since little is available along the way. You can surely find something you like at F. H. Gillingham & Sons (16 Elm Street), founded in 1886 as a general store and now selling gourmet foods, or at one of the many other places in town.

1.0 At the Texaco station (on the right), bear RIGHT off Route 12 toward South Pomfret.

Over the next two miles the road climbs almost imperceptibly, but nevertheless steadily, as it follows Barnard Brook uphill.

2.9 At the Teago General Store in South Pomfret, bear RIGHT toward Pomfret.

The Teago General Store has a selection of beverages, cold cuts, cheeses, and breads. Near the store stands the unconventionally designed Abbott Memorial Library, which contains a museum of local historical memorabilia.

About a mile and a half from South Pomfret, and later near West Hartford, you cross the Appalachian Trail, which runs through southeastern Vermont on its way from Georgia to Maine.

South Pomfret sits at an elevation of 736′ above sea level. Over the next three miles you climb nearly 500 feet—sometimes quite steeply—before reaching Pomfret at 1,200′. This hill presents the most difficult ascent of the tour. From Pomfret you glide downhill seven miles to West Hartford, which lies at an elevation of 420′ on the banks of the White River.

7.8 At Hewetts Corners, continue STRAIGHT. (Maps of the intersection at Hewetts Corners are deceptive. The road you follow through North Pomfret to West Hartford is a continuation of the road from Pomfret, while the road to Sharon branches off to your left and goes toward Interstate 89. Maps make it appear as though the road to West Hartford requires a right turn in Hewetts Corners, but it does not.)

13.0 At the Stop Sign by the bridge outside West Hartford, turn RIGHT onto Quechee-West Hartford Road.

If you are hungry, this is the last place to get food. At this Stop Sign, turn left and ride one-tenth mile across the bridge over the White River to the Stop Sign at Route 14. There, turn left onto Route 14 North and ride two-tenths mile to the West Hartford Country Store on the right.

If you would like to take a swim, the White River is the best place. Assuming you are back at the Stop Sign where you turn right onto Quechee-West Hartford Road, go straight ahead—instead of turning right—onto the small unpaved road and ride a quarter-mile to Erwin Clifford Recreational Park.

Over the next three miles, the Quechee-West Hartford Road climbs out of the White River Valley; so be prepared for the second and final climb of the tour. About two miles before the next turn, the road turns downhill.

18.0 One-tenth of a mile after the inverted Y road sign (on the right), turn sharply RIGHT onto River Road. Approach this turn cautiously, for when you reach it, you are going downhill.

Six-tenths of a mile after turning onto River Road, you pass the Quechee Club on the left. This modern clubhouse on the edge of a new golf course belongs to a major development of opulent condominiums and luxurious recreational facilities.

21.2 Just before the red, Taftsville covered bridge (1836), turn RIGHT onto River Road, which is unpaved and may be unsigned. From this turn to the next find your way by following the roads that keep the Ottauquechee River on your left.

River Road is unpaved for two and three-tenths miles. While you could return to Woodstock on US 4, I do not recommend it because of the high volume of traffic, narrow road width, and lack of beauty. Although the unpaved road demands more than the usual amount of attention, it is quiet, shaded, and provides a delightful view of the Ottauquechee.

24.2 At the Stop Sign, turn LEFT onto Route 12 South.

Just after you turn onto Route 12, you pass the entrance to the Billings Farm and Museum on the left. Here, on a working dairy farm that milks 80 Jersey cows, is a museum illustrating Vermont life in 1890. The Nineties were a special time. Manufactured goods were displacing hand-crafted ones, and the railroad was tying Vermont farmyards to the markets and manners of the urban Northeast. But the well-worn customs of 200 years were not quickly displaced. The museum reveals the richness and sophistication of Vermont farm life as well as its ordinary details. Displays of a church, a school, and a town meeting are also included.

During the early 19th century Billings Farm was home for the young George Perkins Marsh, whose book, *Man and Nature* (1864) became the bible of the early 20th century conservation movement. The museum is the creation of Laurence and Mary Rockefeller, whose family has owned the farm since 1869. It is open daily, 10:00 a.m. to 4:00 p.m., late May through October. Admission is charged.

24.5 You are back in Woodstock where the tour began.

When you reach Woodstock, consider stretching your legs with a walk along one of the town's short nature trails: Faulkner Trail or Mount Peg Trail. Maps of both are available free from the Chamber of Commerce.

Bicycle Repair Services
The Brick Store, The Green, Strafford, VT (802-765-4441)
The Cyclery Plus, US 4, West Woodstock, VT (802-457-3377)
Omer's & Bob's, Nugget Arcade, Hanover, NH (603-643-3525)
The Pedaler, 5 Allen Street, Hanover, NH (603-643-5271)
White River Schwinn, Main Street, White River Junction, VT (802-295-BIKE)

9

Rivers of Central Vermont:
A two-day tour

The distance and terrain are stated at the beginning of each day's directions.

This tour offers not only fine rural bicycling, but exceptional opportunities to fish, swim, visit sites of historical and architectural interest, and to view the state from the top of a mountain without having to cycle there. Along the way you may either camp or stay at country inns. Starting from Plymouth if you camp and Bridgewater Corners or West Woodstock if you use inns, the route parallels rivers or streams nearly all the way. With the exception of twelve miles on US 4, which can be moderately busy, you follow lightly traveled roads—eight miles of which are unpaved.

On the first day you visit the exquisite village of Woodstock, where the architecture of early Vermont is carefully preserved. On the second you pass the Killington Gondola, which you can take to the top of Vermont's second highest mountain. Later that day you bicycle into the hill town of Plymouth, where Calvin Coolidge spent his boyhood and took his oath as president. Words Coolidge wrote about Plymouth over fifty years ago still fit that hamlet and most of the countryside along this tour: "As I look back on it I constantly think how clean it was. There was little that was artificial. It was all close to nature and in accordance with the ways of nature. The streams ran clear. The roads, the woods, the fields, the people—all were clean. Even when I try to divest it of the halo which I know always surrounds the past, I am unable to create any other impression than that it was fresh and clean." (*Autobiography of Calvin Coolidge*, 1929.)

The tour is designed to suit both cyclists who like to camp and those who prefer to stay at country inns. Accordingly, two sets of mileages are given with the directions: campers' distances are indicated first and below them, in parentheses, are the mileages for cyclists traveling between inns. Regardless of which accommodations you use, you will probably find it convenient to sleep at the trail's head the night before you begin riding. If you camp, you will

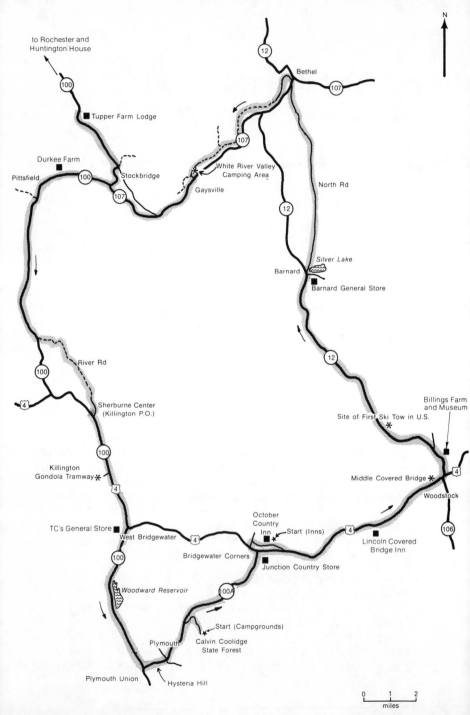

N

to Rochester and
Huntington House

100

■ Tupper Farm Lodge

Bethel

107

■ Durkee Farm

Pittsfield

100

Stockbridge

107

12

White River Valley
Camping Area

Gaysville

North Rd

Silver Lake

Barnard

■ Barnard General Store

River Rd

100

4

Sherburne Center
(Killington P.O.)

12

Site of First Ski Tow in U.S.
*

Billings Farm
and Museum
■

4

100

Killington
Gondola Tramway *

Middle Covered Bridge *

Woodstock

4

106

October
Country
Inn
■ *
Start (Inns)

TC's General Store ■

West Bridgewater

4

4

Lincoln Covered
Bridge Inn
■

100

Bridgewater Corners

Junction Country Store ■

100A

Woodward Reservoir

Start (Campgrounds)

Plymouth

Calvin Coolidge
State Forest

Plymouth Union

Hysteria Hill

0   1   2
miles

save time and eat better by bringing most of your food from home. But whichever way you go, do not set out until you have contacted the places you intend to stay at night, for you cannot rely on their being prepared for you without notice.

The inns on the tour are among my favorite and have delighted many persons who have ridden with Vermont Bicycle Touring. Spend the night before you start cycling at Ruth and Pete Hall's October Country Inn or the Lincoln Covered Bridge Inn. For a year Ruth led tours for Vermont Bicycle Touring, and she knows well the needs of bicyclists. She is one of the finest chefs in Vermont, and the consistently superb meals at the October Country Inn reflect her creative touch. Pete and Ruth have fashioned their cozy, cheerful inn from a nineteenth-century farmhouse. Informal, but gracious, the inn has no rooms with private baths and all guests eat together and bring their own liquor or do without. Ruth and Pete will surely make you feel that this lovely inn, which is their home, is yours too when you are there. Make your reservations by contacting the Halls at October Country Inn, Box 66F, Bridgewater Corners, Vt 05035 (802-672-3412).

If you cannot be accommodated there, try the Lincoln Covered Bridge Inn, which has six pleasant rooms with private baths, a full liquor license, and excellent food, prepared by owner Phil DiPietro. For reservations call (802-457-3312) or write the inn at US 4, West Woodstock, VT 05091. Request one of the rooms that face the river, since they are quieter. By starting at the Lincoln Covered Bridge Inn, you shorten the first day's ride by five miles and lengthen the second by five, for the inn is located on US 4, five miles east of its intersection with Route 100A.

For the night between Days One and Two, the tour goes to Tupper Farm Lodge, Huntington House, or Durkee Farm. There is something magical about Tupper Farm, something that makes every guest feel wonderful but that cannot be fully explained even by its delicious, bountiful meals, comfortable accommodations, and superb swimming hole in the White River. It comes no doubt from the marvelous innkeepers Ann and Roger Verme, but it shall always remain their secret. Like their friends the Halls at October Country Inn, Ann and Roger have created their inn from an old farmhouse (1820). The wallpapered guestrooms share baths; the lodge has no liquor license; and you can expect to join other guests for a candlelit dinner at one large table. After a day's cycling Tupper Farm will immediately put you at ease. The magic will work, and you will know you have come to the right place. You will need a reservation, which you make by contacting Tupper Farm Lodge, Route 100, Box 149F, Rochester, VT 05767 (802-767-4243).

If there is no space at Tupper, try Durkee Farm in Stockbridge or

Huntington House in Rochester. Like October Country Inn and Tupper Farm, Durkee Farm is an informal lodge, set in a refurbished old farmhouse. Innkeepers Dorothy and Bill Doyle are antique dealers as well as good cooks. By staying with them, you shorten your first day's ride by two miles and your second by four. They have seven rooms, some with private bath. For reservations, contact Durkee Farm, Route 100, Stockbridge, VT 05772 (802-746-8141). Huntington House is smaller, more expensive, and more elegant. It opened in 1983 after being completely renovated and furnished with antiques and quilts that match the wallpaper. The food is excellent, and the inn has a full liquor license. One of the five guest rooms has its own bath. Huntington House is attractively located on the east side of the Rochester green; it increases each day's ride by six easy miles. For reservations contact innkeepers David Cayia and Alan Rowe, Huntington House, Box 196, Rochester, VT 05767 (802-767-3511).

For campers the tour starts at Calvin Coolidge State Forest. Its season runs from the Friday before Memorial Day to mid-October. You may rent one of twenty-five tent sites or thirty-five three-sided, wooden floored, ten-by-thirteen-foot lean-tos. Some sites are in designated primitive areas accessible only by foot trail. Hot showers and flush toilets are provided. Vermont state parks do not accept reservations for fewer than three days; campsites are assigned on a first-come, first-served basis. For further information contact Calvin Coolidge State Forest, Plymouth, VT 05056 (802-672-3612).

Campers spend the night between Days One and Two at the White River Valley Camping Area, a member of VAPCOO. Owners Ginny and Denny Merrill have eighty wooded, open, and river sites, and they gladly accept reservations for a single night. Flush toilets, hot showers, a laundromat, firewood, and ice as well as a small store selling mainly canned goods are available. For reservations contact the White River Valley Camping Area, Box 74, Gaysville, VT 05746 (802-234-9115).

Day One

Plymouth to Gaysville (Campgrounds): Moderate terrain; 36.5 miles
Bridgewater Corners to Rochester (Inns): Moderate terrain; 39.5 miles

0.0 At the exit from Calvin Coolidge State Forest turn RIGHT onto Route
— 100A North.

Route 100A runs downhill along Broad Brook for four miles and then flattens out a mile before Bridgewater Corners.

5.0   At the Stop Sign at Bridgewater Corners turn RIGHT onto US 4 East.
(0.0) If you are starting from the October Country Inn, turn LEFT onto US 4
East.

At the intersection of US 4 and Route 100A, you can pick up
supplies at the Junction Country Store. Owners Bob and
Debbie Rice have catered to the needs of bicyclists for many
years and can help you quickly select what you need. Their store
features a broad selection of country wares as well as fresh
meats, cheese, groceries, beverages, and penny candy. During
the 1850s placer gold was discovered in Broad Brook above
Bridgewater Corners. Something of a gold rush ensued, and
there was a lot of panning and digging, but little gold turned
up.

For the next eight miles you follow the Ottauquechee River, a
good trout stream. US 4 often draws a substantial amount of
traffic, though it is not usually bothersome in the morning. Pay
careful attention to your cycling, especially where the road is
narrow. Five miles east of Bridgewater Corners you pass the
Lincoln Covered Bridge Inn on the right and the Lincoln
covered bridge, which stretches 136 feet across the Ottauquechee River. Constructed in 1865, the year of Lincoln's
assassination, this bridge remains Vermont's only example of a
Pratt type truss.

13.0   At the intersection in the center of Woodstock, turn LEFT onto Route
(8.0) 12 North.

Woodstock possesses a wealth of early nineteenth-century
architectural grace. Stately public buildings and fine brick and
clapboard townhouses, built one hundred fifty years ago,
surround an unusual oval green. Woodstock has maintained its
beauty and sustained its prosperity by pursuing finance and
commerce, rather than manufacturing. Perhaps its former residents protected the village from change; certainly the current
ones try to. Telephone and electrical lines are buried; the
exteriors of most buildings have been kept original; and in 1969,
when another bridge was needed to cross the Ottauquechee,
the town built an authentic covered bridge without a nail in it.

Steadfastly reserved, urbane, wealthy, and exclusive, Woodstock
appeals to people of like qualities and in turn provides them with
expensive shops, gracious clubs, and a village of visual
charm. Four churches—the First Congregational (1807), St.
James (1907), the Universalist (1835), and the Masonic Temple,
formerly Christian Church (1827)—still ring bells cast by Paul
Revere. You can probably acquire a better understanding of

Woodstock in a brief time by visiting the Woodstock Historical Society than by doing anything else. In the elegant former residence (1807) of neurologist Charles L. Dana, the Society exhibits a fine collection of early nineteenth-century furnishings including portraits, silver, quilts, locally made furniture, doll houses, and farm implements as well as old historical records and etchings by John Taylor Arms. Behind the house beautiful gardens lead down to the Ottauquechee. The Society is located at 26 Elm Street and open from Memorial Day through October, Monday through Saturday, 11:00 a.m. to 5:00 p.m., and Sunday, 2:00 p.m. to 5:00 p.m. Admission is charged.

During Vermont's warm months Woodstock produces many special events, including an antique automobile rally, a major AKC dog show, and several art and craft exhibits. Information about these and other events can be obtained from the Woodstock Chamber of Commerce, which also publishes an annotated map of the village. You may get a map free at the information booth on the green or the Chamber's office at 4 Central Street.

On the right-side of Route 12, a quarter-mile north of Woodstock, is the Billings Farm and Museum. This working dairy farm and museum depicts Vermont life of the 1890s. The museum is open daily 10:00 a.m. to 4:00 p.m., late May through October. Admission is charged.

Along Route 12, about four miles north of Woodstock, you pass a state historical sign marking a spot of enormous significance to Vermont. In 1934, on a sloping sheep pasture here, two ingenious Yankees hitched a rope to the engine of a Model T Ford to create the first ski tow in America. Now more than forty ski areas operate in Vermont alone, accommodating in a single season seven times the state's population. Just beyond the site of the tow, you cross the Appalachian Trail, which runs from Maine to Georgia. Route 12 then turns uphill, presenting a long and sometimes arduous climb. A level respite of a half-mile divides the winding grade into two parts, each a mile and three-quarters long. The first ascent remains gradual; the second, ending by a room-sized quartz boulder on the right, starts gently, but quickly grows steep. Over the four miles you gain roughly 850' in elevation. But with that climb you complete the hard work of the day and descend rapidly two miles into Barnard.

23.0 At Barnard, do not curve left to follow Route 12 North; instead go **(18.0)** STRAIGHT off Route 12 onto North Road.

Barnard makes an ideal place to picnic and swim. The Barnard

General Store stocks an ample selection of food and also runs a lunch counter where you can get hot soup and cooked meals. Across from the store, a lawn by the shore of Silver Lake provides a perfect place to stretch out, have lunch, and enter the water for a swim. If you are headed for the campground, the Barnard Store is a reliable place to get supplies, and, if you are bound for Tupper Farm Lodge or Durkee Farm, you can pick up beer or wine. During the 1930s Sinclair Lewis and Dorothy Thompson lived in Barnard, and Thompson is buried in the cemetery here.

North Road runs past the southern tip of Silver Lake, up a short hill and then along a plateau from which you can catch glimpses of the Green Mountains to your left. About three miles from Barnard, the road begins to tilt downward, getting progressively steeper as it approaches Bethel. The last mile is very fast and requires your complete attention; by the time you reach Bethel you have descended over 700'.

29.8 At the Yield Sign outside Bethel, turn RIGHT onto Route 107 East.
(24.8) Bethel was the first town chartered by the Republic of Vermont during its fourteen years as an independent nation, 1777-91. The route does not go into the village, and there is no reason to ride there unless you need supplies.

30.5 After crossing a bridge and just before Route 107 goes beneath an
(25.5) underpass, turn LEFT onto the very small, unsigned road.
In a mile and a quarter this road becomes unpaved for four miles. The surface remains hard and smooth for three miles, but becomes slightly soft near the end, when you must climb a half-mile hill.

34.8 At the fork, where the road is still unpaved, bear LEFT so you cross a
(29.8) very small bridge.
In nine-tenths mile, the road becomes paved.

36.3 One-half mile after the pavement resumes, at the bottom of a short hill,
(31.3) turn LEFT and cross the green iron bridge into Gaysville, which consists of a church and tiny post office.
The day's second superb swimming spot lies directly below this bridge in the White River. One of the principal tributaries of the Connecticut River, the White runs approximately sixty miles from Battell Mountain (el. 3471'), west of Granville, to White River Junction. Its wonderfully clear waters provide not only exceptional swimming, but fine cover for trout—especially rainbows and browns—and excellent, though strenuous, white-water canoeing.

The cottage where President Calvin Coolidge was born in 1872 as seen through the window of the Union Christian Church.

36.5 The driveway to the White River Valley Camping area, the end of the
(31.5) day's ride for campers, begins on your left immediately after the green
bridge.

— At the Stop Sign just beyond the Gaysville post office (on the left), turn
(31.6) RIGHT onto Route 107 West.
In three miles Route 107 runs uphill for a half-mile.

— At the intersection of Routes 107 and 100, turn RIGHT onto Route 100
(36.0) North.
If you are headed for Durkee Farm, do not turn right; instead, turn
left onto Route 100 South and ride 1.5 miles to Durkee Farm on
your right.

— At the blinker in Stockbridge, turn LEFT to continue north on Route
(37.2) 100.

— Tupper Farm Lodge stands on your right facing Route 100.
(39.5) If you are staying at Huntington House, continue northward on Route
100 for 6.0 miles to the village of Rochester. Huntington House sits
beside other green shuttered houses on the northeast corner of the
green.

Day Two

**Gaysville to Plymouth (Campgrounds): Moderate terrain; 29
miles
Rochester to Bridgewater Corners (Inns): Moderate terrain; 33
miles**

0.0 From the White River Valley Camping Area, turn LEFT out of the
— driveway onto the unsigned road.

0.1 At the Stop Sign, just beyond the Gaysville post office (on the left),
— turn RIGHT onto Route 107 West.
In three miles Route 107 runs uphill for a half-mile.

— From Tupper Farm Lodge, turn LEFT onto Route 100 South.
(0.0)
— At the blinker in Stockbridge, turn RIGHT to continue south on Route
(2.3) 100.

4.5 At the intersection of Routes 107 and 100, go STRAIGHT onto Route
(3.5) 100 South.
On a clear day you can catch a glimpse of Killington Peak
directly ahead of you. Four miles south of the village of Pittsfield
you begin climbing a relentless grade which in two miles takes
you up 550' in elevation. It is definitely the hardest part of the
day.

12.9 Beside a large, yellow traffic arrow that points to the right, turn LEFT
(11.9) off Route 100 onto River Road, which is unpaved for the first three
and three-quarters miles.

> The surface of River Road is hard and generally free of rocks, but
> ride very cautiously on the downhill sections.

17.0 At the Stop Sign in Sherburne Center (Killington P.O.), turn LEFT onto
(16.0) Route 100 South, which here runs concurrently with US 4 East.
> Over the next four miles you encounter more traffic than you
> have seen since leaving Woodstock. But the road is wide,
> straight, and most of the way offers a shoulder suitable for
> cycling.

> In two miles, at the end of Sherburne flats, you reach the
> Killington Gondola Tramway, the world's longest ski lift. The
> three-and-a-half-mile ride is exciting and worthwhile on a clear
> day. The views from the top are spectacular, and you can enjoy
> them while having lunch at the Peak Restaurant.

> If you can, take along a map to orient yourself and identify the
> major geological formations visible in five states: Vermont, Maine,
> New Hampshire, New York, and Massachusetts. From the gon-
> dola you can walk along a short trail to the top of Killington Peak
> (el. 4,235'), Vermont's second tallest mountain. The tramway oper-
> ates daily from mid-June to late October between 10:00 a.m. and
> 4:00 p.m.; on Wednesday through Sunday evenings it also makes
> sunset trips. Just beyond the gondola, Route 100 dives downhill
> for a mile into West Bridgewater.

21.4 At the blinker in West Bridgewater, turn RIGHT onto Route 100
(20.4) South.
> TC's General Store, to your right at this intersection, makes good
> fresh sandwiches and sells all you need for a picnic. A half-mile
> south of the store, Route 100 starts up a gradual grade that grows
> steeper before ending in a mile and a half at the foot of Woodward
> Reservoir.

26.4 In Plymouth Union, turn LEFT onto Route 100A North.
(25.4) Immediately upon making this turn, you face one of Vermont's
> most formidable short ascents. Fondly and not-so-fondly called
> Hysteria Hill by many bicyclists, this climb, though barely a half-
> mile long, tests the stamina and will of all who try it. But doubtless it
> merits the effort, for it brings an unspoiled downhill run of more
> than five miles. Of course, if you began this tour at Calvin
> Coolidge State Forest, you already benefited from four of those
> miles.

27.4 Four-tenths of a mile beyond the crest of Hysteria Hill and just past a
(26.4) pond on your right, turn LEFT off Route 100A onto the road toward
Plymouth and ride a quarter-mile to that village.

Plymouth deserves a visit for both aesthetic and historical
reasons. Consisting only of a few trim nineteenth-century
clapboard buildings and surrounded by hills, this tiny hamlet
radiates peacefulness and security. Here, at three o'clock on an
August morning in 1923, Vice-president Calvin Coolidge was
awakened to be told that President Harding had died. Then, by
the glow of a kerosene lamp, the most modern form of lighting in
the house, Coolidge took the presidential oath from his father, a
notary public. Fifty-one years earlier on Independence Day
Coolidge was born here in a weathered cottage beside the
church where his family worshipped.

Now a state historic site, Plymouth merits a leisurely visit. The
Coolidge family home, where the vice-president was vacationing when Harding died, has been painstakingly restored to its
condition on that eventful night. In like manner the room where
Coolidge was born has been refurbished as the nineteenth-
century borning room that it was. Along with the Wilder House,
where the president's mother lived until she married, these
buildings accurately portray a style of life common in Vermont
nearly a century ago. Still more can be learned about those
times by visiting the immense old barn that now houses the
Vermont Farmers Museum. Its collection of hand-wrought farm
implements dramatically illustrates the hardship farm families
endured and the ingenious ways they accomplished with
animal and human power tasks now performed by electricity
and internal combustion engines. From late May till mid-
October these buildings are open to the public daily, 9:30 a.m. to
5:30 p.m. Admission is charged.

Plymouth's Union Christian Church (1840), originally Congregational, illustrates the blending of mid- and late-nineteenth century
architecture. The exterior remains unchanged since its construction and resembles that of many other clapboard meetinghouses
around the state. But in 1890 the congregation decided to re-
place the original box pews with a more up-to-date arrangement.
Accordingly they hired a master carpenter who refashioned the
interior out of rare hard pine in a style known as Carpenter Gothic.
This style achieves in wood the Gothic forms usually shaped by
masonry. The church holds services during July and August at
11:00 a.m. on Sundays. The Calvin Coolidge Memorial Center
(1972) houses a collection of Coolidge memorabilia, including

many old photographs captioned with excerpts from his auto-biography. Finally, the Plymouth Cheese Corporation at the northern end of the village makes a unique curd cheese. On weekdays you can watch the process, and every day of the week you can sample the cheese and buy it.

27.9 Retrace your way out of Plymouth and turn LEFT onto Route 100A
(26.9) North toward Woodstock.

29.0 The entrance to Calvin Coolidge State Forest is on your right, where, if you have been camping, you started this tour.

— At the Stop Sign in Bridgewater Corners, turn LEFT onto US 4 West,
(33.0) ride two tenths of a mile, and turn RIGHT toward Bridgewater Center. Go fifty yards, turn RIGHT onto the unpaved road, and ride another one hundred fifty yards to October Country Inn, where you started.

If you began at the Lincoln Covered Bridge Inn, you must turn RIGHT at the Stop Sign in Bridgewater Corners onto US 4 West and ride 5.0 miles. The inn will then be on your right.

Bicycle Repair Services
The Brick Store, The Green, Strafford, VT (802-765-4441)
The Cyclery Plus, US4, West Woodstock, VT (802-457-3377)
Green Mountain Schwinn Cyclery, 133 Strongs Avenue, Rutland, VT (802-775-0869)
Omer's & Bob's, Nugget Arcade, Hanover, NH (603-643-3525)
Sports Peddler, 158 N. Main Street (US 7), Rutland, VT (802-775-0101)
The Pedaler, 5 Allen Street, Hanover, NH (603-643-5271)
White River Schwinn, Main Street, White River Junction, VT (802-295-BIKE)

10

South Royalton–Strafford

Moderate–to–difficult terrain; 28 miles

With the exception of the Northeast Kingdom, fifty to seventy-five miles further north, Orange County may be Vermont's most unspoiled region. It has no ski areas, no major lakes, no cities, and no major mountains. Even Vermont's two Interstate highways, 89 and 91, which enclose this unheralded county on its south, east, and west, seem to funnel the traffic by. And yet Orange County is a wonderland of wooded hills and scenic river valleys, ideal for bicycling. This tour begins in South Royalton and follows untrafficked roads along the First and West Branches of the White River as well as the White River itself. Carving a circle through the tiny villages of South Strafford, Strafford, and Tunbridge, the tour brings excellent views down the valleys and across the rounded hills that feed their streams into the rivers below. Though the route is emphatically pastoral, you have opportunities to see three covered bridges and the magnificent mid-nineteenth-century home of Justin Morrill. If you make the tour in mid-September, you can also join the spirited whirl of the Tunbridge World's Fair.

0.0   Leave South Royalton by riding east on South Windsor Street, the unsigned road running along the northern side of the green.
Founded in 1972, Vermont Law School, the state's first, stands near the green in an old elementary school. A private, three-year institution, the law school enrolls approximately 350 men and women. In Vermont an aspiring lawyer may also gain admission to the bar by reading law with a practicing attorney and then taking the state bar examination. The Royalton Historical Society Museum, located in the 1840 Town House, contains articles relating to the 1780 Royalton Indian raid (led by an English lieutenant) as well as photographs, broadsides, maps, and other possessions of the town's early residents. The museum opens by appointment only (802-763-8567). During the summer on Thursday evenings the South Royalton Band performs on the green. South Windsor Street parallels the White River, which along this stretch offers good swimming and excellent fishing for brown and rainbow trout.

4.7   At the Stop Sign just after you cross an iron bridge outside Sharon, turn RIGHT onto Route 14 South.

5.0   In Sharon, turn LEFT onto Route 132 East toward Strafford and South Strafford.

Joseph Smith, founder of the Church of Jesus Christ of Latter-Day Saints, the Mormons, was born in 1805 on an outlying Sharon farm. Smith lived there until he was ten and received his first visitation four years later in New York. About five miles from this intersection, at the end of a two-mile climb up an unpaved road off Route 14, a quiet retreat has been built at Smith's birthplace. A monolith of Barre granite, 38½ feet high, weighing thirty-nine tons—purportedly the world's largest—marks the site.

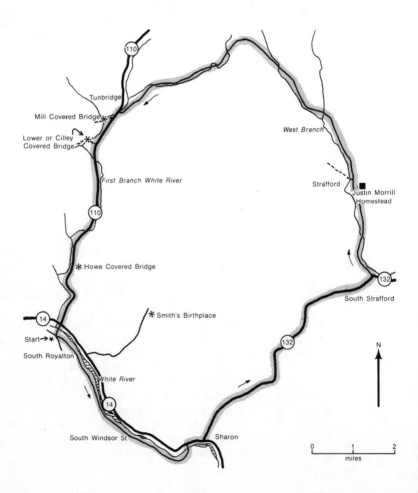

Each foot of the obelisk represents a year in the life of the prophet, who was lynched by a mob in the Carthage, Illinois, jail in 1844. Had it not been for the organizational genius of another Vermonter, Brigham Young, born in Whitingham, Mormonism might have died with Smith.

Within a quarter-mile Route 132 tips sharply uphill for a mile and a quarter, levels off for three-quarters, and then rises steeply again for a mile and a half. At the top, you start down a glorious two-mile descent. Initially the slope is extremely steep so take it cautiously and enjoy the views.

11.4 At the Stop Sign in South Strafford, turn LEFT off Route 132 toward Strafford.

If you want groceries, which are not available again until Tunbridge, turn RIGHT instead of left at this Stop Sign and ride two hundred yards to Coburns' General Store. For seven miles from South Strafford you follow the West Branch of the White River.

In two miles you reach Strafford, where problems with your bicycle can be remedied at The Brick Store, a fine bicycle shop open from 10:00 a.m. to 6:00 p.m., Tuesday through Saturday.

You might also enjoy pausing in Strafford to visit the striking, 17-room American Gothic homestead Justin S. Morrill had built for himself from 1848 to 1851. Now a state historic site and National Register Property, the brick and stone building is open daily except Mondays from late May until early September. Morrill, who represented Vermont in the U.S. House and Senate for forty-three years, was born in Strafford. He is known best for the Morrill Act passed during the Civil War. It granted each loyal state federal land for the support of colleges that would teach agriculture and the mechanic arts. Under this act and its successors states received 17,400,000 acres of land—nearly three times the area of Vermont—and by 1961 sixty-nine land-grant colleges had been established. The Morrill Act underwrote the first major practical and technical programs of study in American higher education, previously the exclusive bastion of classical studies in arts, sciences, and languages.

The white meeting house that stands on a hill in the center of Strafford was built in 1779 and is reputed to be the oldest Universalist Church in the country. On the green near The Brick Store is The Stone Soup Ice Cream Parlor, open Saturdays and Sundays from noon until dark. Behind the ice cream parlor is a small antique shop open at the same times.

Strafford Meeting House (1779), the oldest Universalist Church in America.

13.4 Just after passing the Town Clerk's office and The Brick Store (both on the left) in Strafford, bear RIGHT toward Chelsea and Tunbridge so you pass the green and meeting house on your left.

Just beyond Strafford you start up a gradual but steady grade that gets steeper as you go and reaches the crest of the tour's last climb in slightly over four miles. Trees shade the road most of the way, but you have a fine view of the surrounding hills from the top. Then the road drops steeply into a fast three-and-a-half-mile run into Tunbridge.

21.7 At the Stop Sign in Tunbridge, turn LEFT onto Route 110 South.

For over a century Tunbridge has been celebrating the World's Fair of the Union Agricultural Society in mid-September. Sometimes drawing 15,000 persons a day, the four-day festival blends the exuberant spirit of a carnival with the exhibits and competitions of an agricultural fair. Folklore says that in years past all sober persons were herded off the grounds at three in the afternoon as undesirables. Others say the bacchanalian tradition continues. In any case, if you arrive during the fair, judge for yourself and watch the traffic carefully. Information about the official events can be obtained from the Town Clerk, Tunbridge, VT 05077 (802-889-5521).

Within a tenth of a mile after you start south on Route 110, you can see the Mill covered bridge. Built across the First Branch of the White River in 1883, its structure is Multiple Kingpost, having a span of sixty feet. Just beyond the bridge, you can buy groceries at the Tunbridge Village Store. A mile further south, if you turn off Route 110 onto the unpaved road which enters from the west, you can find the Lower or Cilley covered bridge. This bridge, also built in 1883, measures sixty-five feet. Three miles later, the sixty-foot Howe covered bridge, built in 1879, comes into view on your left. Route 110 slopes slightly downward nearly the entire way, as it follows the First Branch of the White River seven miles to South Royalton.

27.7 At the Stop Sign at the intersection of Routes 110 and 14, go STRAIGHT across Route 14 onto the road to South Royalton.

28.0 You enter South Royalton along the west side of the green, where the tour began.

Bicycle Repair Services
The Brick Store, The Green, Strafford, VT (802-765-4441)
The Cyclery Plus, US 4, West Woodstock, VT (802-457-3377)
Omer's & Bob's, Nugget Arcade, Hanover, NH (603-643-3525)
The Pedaler, 5 Allen Street, Hanover, NH (603-643-5271)
White River Schwinn, Main Street, White River Junction, VT (802-295-BIKE)

11

Randolph–Brookfield

Moderate terrain; 38 miles

A quiet valley along the Third Branch of the White River and a moderately hilly ridge overlooking the Green Mountains are the principal geographical features that define this tour. It is emphatically pastoral, and yet there are many places of interest along the way. Randolph is the home of Vermont Castings, one of the world's leading manufacturers of cast-iron stoves, and you can visit its showroom. Fine swimming will tempt the most persistent cyclists—at a waterfall and in a clear, deep lake. On the fringe of the tour stand two small colleges, one a military academy and the other a technical school. For dining the area offers two charming inns—one on a Morgan horse farm and one beside Vermont's only floating bridge. The terrain is accurately categorized as moderate—about nine and a half miles are uphill—but it may seem more difficult, for all the climbing comes in the final third of the tour.

0.0   From the railroad tracks in the center of Randolph, follow Route 12 North, also called North Main Street.

Randolph sits along the Third Branch of the White River at an altitude of 694′, the lowest point on the tour.

The economy and appearance of Randolph have improved greatly since 1975 when Vermont Castings was founded. Now employing 500 persons and annually producing 50,000 cast-iron stoves, this firm is publicly "committed to a conservation ethic that mandates the wise use of wood and coal as a viable alternative to exhausting the earth's energy reserves. A natural extension of this belief tells us that a well-made, durable product, as opposed to one of short life which must be replaced and remanufactured, is another sensible way to save our natural resources." The stoves made by Vermont Castings are beautiful as well as efficient. A showroom on Prince Street is open to the public, Monday through Friday, 9:00 a.m. to 5:00 p.m. and Saturday from 8:00 a.m. to 4:00 p.m.

0.3   At the T beside Victoria's Restaurant, on the left, turn LEFT onto Route 12A North, also called Park Street.

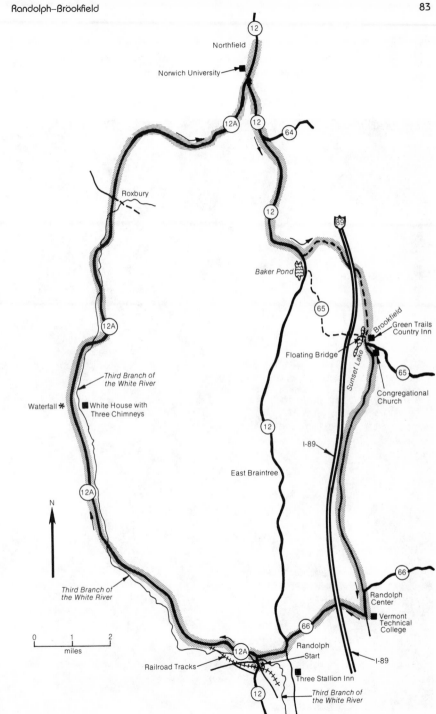

Northfield

Norwich University

12A

12

64

Roxbury

12

I-89

Baker Pond

65

Brookfield
Green Trails
Country Inn

12A

Floating Bridge

Sunset Lake

65

Third Branch of
the White River

Congregational
Church

Waterfall ✱ ■ White House with
Three Chimneys

12

I-89

East Braintree

N

12A

Third Branch of
the White River

66

Randolph
Center

Vermont
Technical
College

0   1   2
miles

66

Railroad Tracks

12A

Randolph
Start

I-89

Three Stallion Inn

12

Third Branch of
the White River

Route 12A makes easy cycling as it follows the Third Branch of
the White River. In about nine and a half miles, consider taking a
walk into the woods to a sparkling thirty-foot waterfall. Stop
beside a white house with three chimneys on the right. Follow

the path across the road from the house uphill into the woods. It is a delightful 150-yard walk along the stream to the falls.

21.3 At the intersection, turn sharply RIGHT onto Route 12 South.

If you need food, you can find it in Northfield by riding one mile north on Route 12, instead of going immediately south. North-field is the home of Norwich University (1819), a private, coeducational college of 1,000 cadets that is probably the oldest private military academy in the U.S. Norwich sent over 300 officers to fight in the Civil War. In 1867 the college moved from Norwich, Vermont, to its present location.

The handsome Northfield common sits at an altitude of 760', well below Brookfield at 1481'. Obviously the next seven miles are going to pose considerable challenge as Route 12 goes steadily uphill.

25.4 Beside a green sign, on the left, that reads "Brookfield and the Brook-field Floating Bridge," turn LEFT onto the unpaved road.
Most of the way to Brookfield is still uphill! In a mile and three-quarters, the road becomes paved. Nine-tenths mile further on, it goes through an underpass beneath Interstate 89.

If you miss the turn to Brookfield, you will reach Baker Pond on your right in a quarter-mile and then Route 65 on your left. Though Route 65 does go to Brookfield, do not take it. In this area it is an unpleasant road for bicycling.

28.2 At the fork, bear RIGHT onto the unsigned road.
In two-tenths mile this road becomes unpaved. A quarter-mile later, it turns steeply downhill for three-tenths of a mile. Ride very cautiously.

29.1 At the Stop Sign in Brookfield, go STRAIGHT onto Route 65 East, though there may not be a route marker there.
For a tenth of a mile Route 65 is not paved.

The current floating bridge—50 feet to your right when you reach this Stop Sign—is actually the seventh such structure to span the 320 feet across Sunset Lake (also called Clinton and Mirror Pond). The first was built in approximately 1820, and it and its successors were essentially rafts buoyed up by empty wooden maple syrup, or later kerosene, barrels. When heavy traffic crossed the bridge, it sank beneath the surface of the pond. The present bridge, constructed in 1978, floats on polyethylene bar-rels that are filled with polystyrene. Some people claim that a floating bridge is used here—and it is the only one in Vermont—because the pond is too deep to support a pillared span. Others claim that a tradition is a tradition, and Brookfield simply wouldn't be Brookfield if the bridge didn't float! In any case the swimming and fishing off the bridge are excellent.

The charming Green Trails Country Inn—immediately on your left when you reach the Stop Sign in Brookfield—offers attractive accommodations and a warm welcome. Innkeepers Betty and Jack Russell serve homemade breakfasts and dinners; call ahead (802-276-3412).

29.3 At the white Brookfield Congregational Church, just after Route 65 becomes paved again, turn RIGHT off Route 65 onto Ridge Road toward Brookfield Center. There may not be a street sign here. For the next three miles the road rolls up and down short moderately steep hills.

35.9 At the Yield Sign in Randolph Center, go STRAIGHT onto Route 66 West, which is unsigned here.

Most activity in Randolph Center revolves around Floyd's General Store and Vermont Technical College. The latter enrolls 750 men and women who are studying for associate degrees in agriculture, business, and engineering.

Randolph Center is also the original home of that especially American horse, the Morgan, for it was here that Justin Morgan and his small, rough-coated colt, Figure, settled in 1795. Now Vermont's state animal, the Morgan horse is extolled for the diversity of its abilities. It can be a cowhorse, pleasure horse, equitation horse, or harness horse. The Vermont Morgan Horse Farm in Weybridge is on the Middlebury–Vergennes tour.

36.7 At the Stop Sign, turn RIGHT to continue on Route 66 West toward Randolph.

The next three miles descend rapidly back into Randolph. In two and three-quarter miles, if you turn left onto Stockfarm Road and ride six-tenths mile to the Three Stallion Inn, you can complete your day with cocktails and dinner in a lovely spot, overlooking the paddocks of a well-groomed horsefarm. Innkeepers Roxanne and Tom Sejerman are delightful hosts.

37.3 At the Traffic light in Randolph, bear LEFT onto Route 12 South, also called Forest Street.

Beware of the traffic at this intersection.

37.5 At the intersection beside Victoria's Restaurant, turn LEFT to continue on Route 12 South toward Bethel and Rutland.

You are back in the center of the village where this tour originated.

Bicycle Repair Services
The Brick Store, The Green, Strafford, VT (802-765-4441)
The Cyclery Plus, US 4, West Woodstock, VT (802-457-3377)
Demers Repairs, Inc., 81 South Main Street, Barre, VT (802-476-7712)
Onion River Sports, 20 Langdon Street, Montpelier, VT (802-229-9409)

12
Fairlee–Haverhill (N.H.)

Easy-to-moderate terrain; 26 or 17 miles

This tour sits in a cycling paradise where Vermont and New Hampshire meet. Only seventeen miles north of Hanover, the tour presents an entertaining potpourri of historic architecture, lovely lakes, river views, prosperous farmland, a nationally prominent Model A garage, and more. Since the cycling is neither difficult nor long, by making a day of it, you will have ample time to enjoy what you find along the way. And, when you're through, consider stopping in Hanover to explore the campus of Dartmouth College (1769), visit the shop of the League of New Hampshire Craftsmen, and treat yourself to some freshly made ice cream at The Ice Cream Machine.

0.0 From the green in Fairlee, ride south on US 5.

Afficionados of road food as well as hungry bicyclists find themselves at home and well-fed at the Fairlee Diner, here on US 5. It is a living artifact from the time when travelers drove on roads, rather than superhighways. This area of the upper Connecticut River Valley between Hanover and Haverhill has an abundance of lodges and inns. My favorite is Loch Lyme Lodge in Lyme, New Hampshire, six miles south of Fairlee. It has splendid swimming, homecooked meals, and rustic cabins with fireplaces and porches.

0.3 Turn RIGHT toward Interstate 91.

0.5 Go STRAIGHT onto Lake Morey West Road which follows the lake's western shore; in other words the water will be on your right.

The lake is named after Samuel Morey, who lived in Fairlee and Orford, New Hampshire, in the late 18th century. He invented many things and in 1826 patented an internal combustion engine. It also seems possible that Morey invented and operated the world's first steamboat. In 1797, ten years before Robert Fulton launched his *Clermont*, Morey was plying the Connecticut River in a comical little craft, barely large enough to carry himself, a steam boiler, and an armful of wood. Morey showed his boat to Fulton, and some local patriots feel that Fulton, whom history honors as the steamboat's creator, received credit for Morey's invention. Morey went on to hitch an internal combustion engine to a little boat, dubbed *Aunt Sally*. Nevertheless, he became discouraged and embittered by his repeated failures to

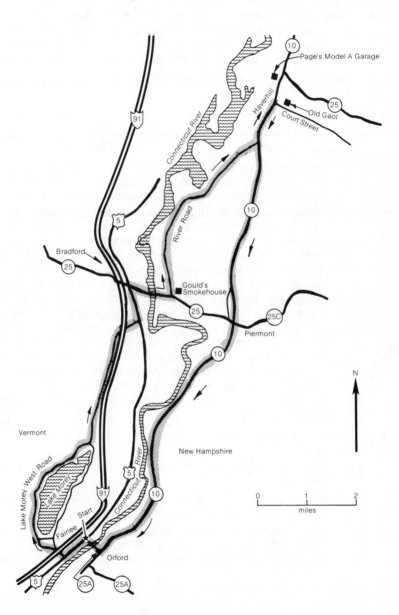

convince the world of the usefulness of his inventions and sank his beloved *Aunt Sally* in Lake Morey. Attempts to locate the venerable boat have proved unsuccessful. Fishing for bass and perch is more promising.

3.5   Turn LEFT onto the first paved road, which is unsigned.
In a half-mile you start the first of two, back-to-back climbs. Each one lasts about five-eighths of a mile; both are quite steep. From the top, the road shoots swiftly downhill for a mile and a half.

6.8   At the Stop Sign, turn LEFT onto US 5 North, which may be unsigned here.

7.4   At the Traffic Light just south of Bradford, turn RIGHT onto Route 25 East, which takes you across the Connecticut River.
Just beyond the river, there's a short climb.

Bradford hosts a traditional country fair and an unusual Wild Game Supper. The Connecticut Valley Fair is held at fairgrounds on US 5, just north of the village on the last full weekend in July. Activities begin on Thursday evening and feature agricultural and homemaking competitions; horse, ox and tractor pulls; carnival rides; and country and western music. The Bradford Wild Game Supper is held at the United Church of Christ on Main Street and takes place on the Saturday before Thanksgiving. The parishioners prepare a gargantuan feast that includes raccoon pie, wild boar sausage, bear roast, venison steak, rabbit liver, buffalo stew, and moose burgers as well as pheasant, Moufflon ram, beaver, salad, vegetables, and gingerbread with whipped cream. There are six seatings, beginning at 2:00 or 3:00, and they consume some 2800 field-dressed pounds of game. Admission is charged to both the fair and the supper. For further information—and you need tickets for the Game Supper—contact the Town Clerk, Bradford, VT 05033, (802-222-4727).

8.5   Four-tenths mile after you cross the river, turn LEFT onto River Road.
Gould's Smokehouse, on your left at this intersection, is a good grocery.

To shorten your ride to 17 miles, do not turn onto River Road. Instead continue STRAIGHT on Route 25 East for 1.9 miles more, about half of which goes uphill. Then at the blinker (in Piermont), turn RIGHT onto New Hampshire Route 10 and ride 6.2 miles to Orford. From there, continue as below from mileage 25.6.

Heading northward on River Road, the cycling is easy until the last mile, which climbs a moderate hill.

12.9 At the Yield Sign, turn LEFT onto Route 10 North, which may be unsigned here.

14.1 The Haverhill green is on your right, and you have reached the northernmost point of the tour. To complete the ride, turn around and head south on Route 10.

Haverhill (1763) is one of the Granite State's most beautiful and uncommercial villages. In the middle of the past century it chose not to have the railroad from Boston come into town. So the tracks were curved northward toward Woodsville which became a commercial center and allowed Haverhill to remain pristine. Exquisite 18th and 19th century homes and public buildings are gathered about two commons. The 18th century jail is now owned by Mr. & Mrs. Clayton Bailwitz, and they welcome cycling visitors. Turn right onto Court Street, which runs eastward between the commons, and ride a quarter-mile to the sixth house on the left. The jail is attached to the back of a white clapboard house, and a sign out front reads Old County Gaol (1794). Haverhill is also home to Page's outstanding Model A garage, a half-mile north of the commons on the west side of Route 10

Though he does not know it yet, the cyclist still riding has just gotten a flat!

across from the post office. At Page's you receive a warm welcome, and can see Model A Fords—and a few V-8s—in every stage of restoration. Page's repairs, restores, and sells parts for Henry Ford's Model A, ever-popular, though manufactured for only four years, 1928–31. Page's Garage is open weekdays from 8:00 a.m. to 5:00 p.m. and Saturdays from 8:00 a.m. to 1:00 p.m.

25.6 In Orford, turn RIGHT onto Route 25A West toward Fairlee, Vermont.

In the early 19th century, after visiting Orford, Washington Irving wrote: "In all my travels in this country and Europe, I have seen no village more beautiful." Orford is no longer the thriving village it was prior to the westward exodus of the 1840s and the industrial revolution which silenced the water-powered mills. But it remains a village of great charm and remarkable architecture. The buildings that line Orford Street compose a district, entered in the National Register of Historic Places. Most prominent are the seven houses, set back from the east side of the road on the Ridge. They date from 1773 to 1840 and were designed by a Boston architect, probably Asher Benjamin, who was a colleague of Charles Bulfinch. Facing the Ridge are John Mann's weathered frame house (1788–1809), Abiathar Britton's brick house (1831), and the Congregational Church (1854), among others.

25.9 At the Stop Sign in Fairlee, turn LEFT onto US 5 South.

26.0 You are again at the green (on your right) in Fairlee.

Bicycle Repair Services
The Brick Store, The Green, Strafford, VT (802-965-4441)
Dion's Ski & Bicycle Shop, 55 Main Street, West Lebanon, NH (603-298-8051)
Ed's Bike & Sports Shop, 61C Hanover Street, Lebanon, NH (603-448-1125)
Littleton Bicycle Shop, 126½ Main Street, Littleton, NH (603-444-3437)
Omer's & Bob's, Nugget Arcade, Hanover, NH (603-643-3525)
The Pedaler, 5 Allen Street, Hanover, NH (603-643-5271)
Thomas Chamberlain, Main Street, Newbury, VT (802-866-5916)
Tom Mowatt Cycles, 3 High Street, Lebanon, NH (603-448-5556)
US Ski & Sport Shop, Main Street, Lincoln, NH (603-745-8831)
White River Schwinn, Main Street, White River Junction, VT (802-295-BIKE)

13

Rutland–North Shrewsbury

Difficult terrain; 24 Miles

This tour dramatizes the remarkable spaciousness and pastoral nature of Vermont. Though it starts near the center of the state's second largest city, the tour follows main roads for only one out of twenty-four miles. The remainder lie in remote hills quilted with stands of birch, sugarmaples, and evergreens; views of some of the Green Mountains highest peaks are stupendous. Often you can hear the Cold River bubbling alongside the road, and two covered bridges, each over a century-old, are on the fringe of the route. At the tour's end, though you are merely a mile from the Rutland State Airport, you have no sense that it is there as you follow a quiet farming valley that looks across hilltops to the sunset.

Consider doing the Rutland–North Shrewsbury tour in two directions. As I have written it, you climb to North Shrewsbury on the more gradual, but longer, approach. Try that one in the spring; then return in autumn—if you wait until the leaves have fallen, the views are even more spectacular—and tackle the climb from the steeper side.

0.0   From the Traffic Light on US 7 by Ames/Finast Shopping Center, one and three quarters miles south of US 4, turn LEFT onto US 7 North.

US 7 is the main north-south artery in western Vermont. Fortunately, in this area, the highway has a shoulder suitable for cycling.

With a population of 19,000, Rutland ranks as Vermont's second largest city. Though it lacks the vigor and luster of Burlington—the state's largest city, as well as its medical, cultural, and commercial center—Rutland has its share of attractions. The heart of the city lies just west and south of the intersection of US 7 and US 4. Early Victorian mansions there evoke images of Rutland's nineteenth century prosperity, when it was known as "the marble city." That accolade derives from the great marble deposits stretching from Rutland southward. The first commercial marble quarry in America was established just thirty miles away in Dorset in 1758; see the Dorset–Manchester tour. The

Vermont Marble Company Exhibit on Route 3, just three miles northwest of the center of Rutland, is the world's largest depiction of the story of marble from quarry to sculpted work of art. The exhibit is open daily, mid-May to late October, 9:00 a.m. to 5:30 p.m. Admission is charged.

Rutland takes justifiable pride in being the home of the state's oldest and finest newspaper, *The Rutland Herald* (1794). *The Herald* provides exceptional national and international news coverage for a rural daily and carries many *New York Times* features. One of New England's largest and most interesting traders in used and rare books, Charles E. Tuttle Company, faces the city park at 28 South Main Street (US 7). Four doors

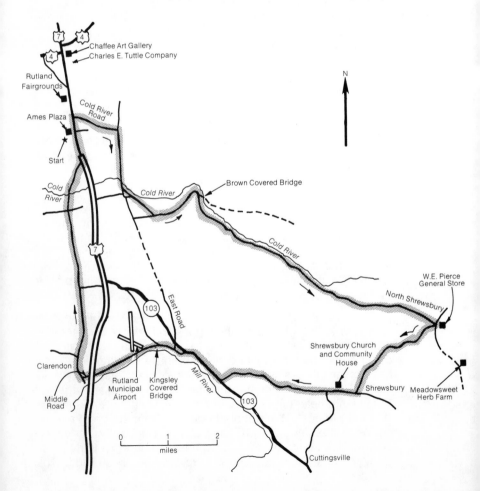

north at 16 South Main is the Chaffee Art Gallery, which is listed in the National Register of Historic Places. It displays both permanent and changing exhibits of painting, sculpture, photography, and crafts. The gallery is open Monday through Friday, 10:00 a.m. to 5:00 p.m., June through October, and weekends by appointment (802-775-0356).

If you seek more frenetic entertainment, try the Vermont State Fair, which runs just one week a year, beginning on the Saturday before Labor Day. The Fair, which has its own fairgrounds on US 7 three-quarters of a mile north of where this tour starts, features daredevil and rodeo events, carnival booths, and harness racing, as well as livestock and agricultural exhibits. Rutland is also "The Gateway City" to the immense skiing operation at Killington and the smaller one at Pico. For further information about continuing and special events stop at the marble information booth in the park on South Main Street or contact the Rutland Chamber of Commerce, Box 27, Rutland, VT 05701 (802-773-2747).

0.3   Turn RIGHT onto Cold River Road.
You cross a set of railroad tracks in three-tenths of a mile.

A major climb lies ahead. From 550' at Rutland, you pedal up to 1758' at North Shrewsbury. The grade is gentle-to-moderate most of the way, but several stretches are steep.

1.2   At the Stop Sign, turn RIGHT to continue on Cold River Road, which is unsigned here. Thereafter, follow the main road and signs for Meadowsweet Herb Farm.
In three miles, by a yellow sign on the left that reads 8' 11", an unpaved road forks to your left and leads down to a charming covered bridge. Built in Town Lattice style in 1880, the Brown covered bridge sits in a romantic wooded hollow over the Cold River. The bridge is just a quarter-mile off the route and is in especially good condition.

10.3   At the fork in North Shrewsbury, bear RIGHT toward Meadowsweet Herb Farm.
Don't pass W.E. Pierce General Store (on the left as soon as you turn) without stopping in. It is closed on Sundays. Still run by sons of the man who founded it in 1918, Pierce's Store is one of the most authentically old-fashioned stores in Vermont. There is no other place for food or drink for the next ten miles.

10.4   Seventy-five yards beyond W.E. Pierce General Store, bear RIGHT onto the unsigned road that goes downhill. This time do not turn toward Meadowsweet Herb Farm unless you intend to make a visit.

In fact the farm is well worth visiting. Polly Haynes and her compatriots are busy year-round raising over 175 herbs and scented geraniums and crafting them into herb wreaths, potpourri, and culinary blends. The farm also features gardens modeled after the Italian Renaissance. Meadowsweet Herb Farm is open Monday through Saturday, 10:00 a.m. to 5:00 p.m., and Sunday by appointment (802-492-3566). To reach the farm, turn left here and follow the road one mile—the second half of which is unpaved. The Haynes farmhouse is on the left.

The road the tour follows goes immediately and steeply downhill for a half-mile, turns sharply uphill for the next mile, and then finishes with a merry descent all the way to the next turn.

13.5 A quarter-mile beyond the Shrewsbury Community Church and Meeting House (1804) on the right, go STRAIGHT onto the unsigned road. Do NOT turn left toward Cuttingsville.

You now descend steeply through the woods for three miles. Keep your speed fully under control and be prepared to stop, for the road ends suddenly at a Stop Sign.

15.8 At the Stop Sign, turn RIGHT onto Route 103 North, which may be unsigned here.

In a half-mile you cross the Long Trail which runs 261 miles through the middle of Vermont from Massachusetts to Canada. It was built by the Green Mountain Club between 1910 and 1929.

17.0 Turn LEFT off Route 103 onto the road toward the airport.

17.1 At the T, bear RIGHT to follow the main road.

17.4 At the fork, bear LEFT down the hill.

In fifty yards, on a side road to your left, the 120-foot Kingsley covered bridge, built by T. K. Norton in 1836, spans the Mill River. Fifty yards further on, the road becomes unpaved for one and a third miles until just before the next direction.

18.9 At each of the three Stop Signs, go STRAIGHT in order to cross US 7 onto Middle Road. The street sign is nailed to a tree on the left, and you cannot see it until after you cross US 7.

In four-tenths mile you pass the Old Brick Clarendon Congregational Church on the right. You are now at an elevation of 600'.

19.5 At the fork, bear RIGHT onto the unsigned road.

22.6 At the Stop Sign at the crossroad, go STRAIGHT onto the unsigned road.

23.4 At the Traffic Light, turn LEFT onto US 7 North.

24.2 At the Traffic Light, you are across from Ames/Finast Shopping Center on the left. This is where the tour began.

Bicycle Repair Services

Battenkill Sports, Routes 11 & 30, Manchester Center, VT (802-362-2734)

Green Mountain Schwinn Cyclery, 133 Strongs Avenue, Rutland, VT (802-775-0869)

Sports Peddler, 158 North Main Street (US 7), Rutland, VT (802-775-0101)

14
Waitsfield–Warren

Easy–to–moderate terrain; 16 miles

The Waitsfield–Warren area, known as the Sugarbush* or Mad River Valley, offers some fine cycling amidst the attractions of one of the East's major ski resorts. Starting a half-mile south of Waitsfield, this tour visits two charming villages, each with its own covered bridge, and then explores open countryside at the base of the Lincoln range of the Green Mountains. Recreation has displaced farming and lumbering as the principal business of the Valley, and consequently you can combine this short bicycle tour with other activity, such as a glider or balloon ride out of the Warren airport (802-496-2290), horseback riding at any of several stables, tennis at many inns and hotels, golf at the Robert Trent golf course, or trout fishing in the Mad River. The numerous shops and restaurants along Route 100 at the tour's conclusion will surely satisfy the appetites of the most curious shopper or hungry gourmet. The tour begins at the Mad River Green Shopping Center midway between Irasville and Waitsfield on the northwest side of Route 100, a half-mile north of the intersection of Routes 100 and 17.

0.0   Turn LEFT out of the Mad River Green Shopping Center onto Route 100 North.

Before leaving the shopping center, you might stop at The Breadbasket Bakery to choose some freshly made bread and pastry, cheese, delicatessen cold cuts, or other treats to carry along.

Barely after you have shifted gears for the first time, you reach the Village Square Shopping Center on your right. Stop there at the Information Booth to get a copy of *The Valley Reporter's* free fifty-six-page pamphlet, "The Mad River Valley Vermont." It

---

*Sugarbush is a generic term for any woods of sugar maple trees. The word derives from the time when sap was collected and boiled to make sugar, rather than syrup. The process, which takes place in the early spring, is still called sugaring whether its product is syrup or sugar. The valley and two of its ski areas have taken their names from the stands of sugar maples on Lincoln Peak and the neighboring hills.

provides a wealth of useful information about the natural, recreational, and commercial life of the area. And while you are there, inquire about special events, such as concerts, craft exhibits, fairs, and sporting contests. Should you want further information or wish to make reservations anywhere closeby, take advantage of the hospitality of the tiny Waitsfield—Fayston Telephone Company. You can make local calls free from the public telephones in each of the Waitsfield and Irasville shopping centers as well as in the villages of Waitsfield and Warren. The Cheese Shop in the Village Square purveys a broad selection of local and imported cheeses as well as crackers, wines, and sweets—all of which will taste especially good when you reach the top of the hill outside Waitsfield.

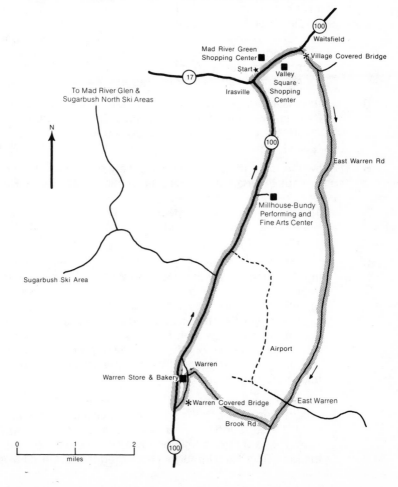

0.8   Just before you pass the Waitsfield Town Library (in a beige, brick building) on the right, turn RIGHT onto East Warren Road so you pass the library on your left. (There may not be a street sign at this intersection, but you are on the course if you cross a covered bridge within a quarter-mile.)

The Village or Big Eddy covered bridge reaches 113 feet over the Mad River. It was built in 1833 and recently restored by Milton Grafton and Sons.

Just beyond the bridge, East Warren Road begins an ascent that is nearly two and a half miles long. The grade is steady but seldom very steep, and it is the only trying climb of the tour.

1.2   At the fork, continue STRAIGHT uphill toward East Warren.

In about a mile and a half, just as the hill ends, the rare, handsome Joslin round barn rises on your left. Constructed in 1910, it is the last round barn left in the Mad River Valley and one of only a few still standing in Vermont. Four and a quarter miles beyond the barn, the road turns downhill making a fast, exhilarating descent for two and a half miles into Warren.

7.0   At the crossroad, go STRAIGHT to continue on East Warren Road.

Off to the west (on your right), the trails of the Sugarbush Ski Area stand out clearly on the wooded slopes of Lincoln Peak (el. 3,975').

7.5   Follow the main road as it curves ninety degrees to the right. (On some maps the road changes name at this point to Brook Road; but in any case there is no street sign.)

The descent gets progressively steeper as you approach Warren. So heed the road signs and ride the last half-mile slowly.

9.3   At the Yield Sign in Warren, turn LEFT onto the unsigned road.

In a hundred yards you reach the Warren Store and Bakery on your right. Located in a former inn and library, the store stocks an attractive variety of foods, which make it a favorite stopping place for cyclists. The breads and sandwiches are excellent as are the wines. Large wooden bins are heaped high with dried fruits, nuts, penny candy, and fresh produce. The balcony upstairs serves as a country boutique selling clothing, fabrics, baskets, and kitchenware.

While you are at the store, get directions to the dam and old abandoned lumber mills south of the village on the Mad River. Until the surrounding area became a downhill skiing center, Warren was a lumber milling town. Just below the dam, where the Mad River cuts through a rocky, jagged gorge, it has carved a natural bridge of stone, called The Arch. If you feel like stretching your legs with a short hike, ask the shopkeepers to point the way to the mile-long trail leading up Lincoln Brook from the old bobbin mill.

As you leave Warren, stop again to look at the Warren covered bridge that Walter Bagley built in 1880 and at the waterfalls below it. Calm and clear above the falls, the Mad River makes excellent swimming here.

10.0 At the Stop Sign, turn RIGHT onto Route 100 North.

The main artery of the Sugarbush Valley, Route 100 connects Warren to Waitsfield and feeds traffic to the valley's three ski areas—Mad River Glen, Sugarbush, and Sugarbush North—and to the summer recreational facilities that have sprung up near them. Consequently the traffic can get heavy, especially in the afternoon during July, August, and early October.

In about three miles, you find the driveway to the Millhouse-Bundy Performing and Fine Arts Center by looking carefully for its sign on your right just after you cross a bridge. The Center's art gallery, which features changing exhibits, is housed in a contemporary building and sits on 350 acres of woods and fields at the end of a half-mile, uphill, unpaved drive. It definitely merits a visit. Large metal and wooden outdoor sculptures are placed dramatically in a serene natural setting, enhanced by open spaces and a man-made duck pond that reflects the mountains. Inside the museum, paintings and more sculpture are displayed. On many Sunday afternoons in July and August, the center presents free outdoor concerts. It is open daily except Wednesday from July through Labor Day between 10:00 a.m. and 5:00 p.m. Admission is free. For scheduling information, call 802-496-3713.

Over the last half-mile of the tour—from the intersection of Routes 100 and 17 north to the Mad River Green Shopping Center—both sides of the road offer an interesting assortment of eateries, shops, and galleries. It would be easy to spend a pleasant afternoon exploring these places and sampling their wares.

16.0   The Mad River Green Shopping Center, where you began, is on the left.

Bicycle Repair Services
Demers Repair, Inc., 81 South Main Street, Barre, VT (802-476-7712)
Inverness Ski and Sports, Mad River Green Shopping Center, Waitsfield, VT (802-496-3343)
Onion River Sports, 20 Langdon Street, Montpelier, VT (802-229-9409)
Vermont Bicycle Touring, Monkton Road, Bristol, VT (802-453-4811)

15

Brandon–Fort Ticonderoga

Moderate–to–difficult terrain; 44 miles

This route highlights Revolutionary history, apple orchards, prosperous dairy farms, and panoramic vistas in the southern Champlain Valley, "Land of Milk and Honey." To maximize the superlative long views of the Adirondack and Green mountains it is best to ride the route on a clear day. Leaving Brandon and then twice crossing the Otter Creek, an important Indian waterway two hundred years ago, you cycle parts of the old Crown Point Military Road, which Lord Jeffrey Amherst cut through the wilderness from Charlestown, New Hampshire, to Lake Champlain in 1759. It was this road that Colonel Henry Knox and his army of farmers used during the winter of 1775 to haul fifty-nine cannons overland from Fort Ticonderoga to Boston, where they played a critical role in expelling the British. The tour merits its moderate-to-difficult rating, because the ride back to Brandon from Fort Ticonderoga is hilly and considerably more demanding than the ride out.

0.0 From the Brandon green ride north on US 7.
US 7 is narrow and heavily traveled in this vicinity.

Brandon was chartered in 1761, and fine post-Revolutionary and Victorian homes line its wide streets. Stephan A. Douglas, "The Little Giant" who, as a Democrat, ran against Abraham Lincoln for the presidency in 1860, was born here in 1813. The story-and-a-half cottage that was his birthplace sits at the northern end of the village, on your left as you leave town on US 7. The cottage now serves the local Daughters of the American Revolution as their headquarters and is open to the public on Thursday afternoons from 2:00 p.m. to 5:00 p.m., June through September.

Douglas and Lincoln differed not about the abolition of slavery—neither at this time favored abolition—but about the question of slavery in U.S. territories. Douglas and the Democrats favored allowing the voters in each territory to decide by ballot whether or not to permit slavery. Lincoln and the Republicans advocated Congressional legislation to prohibit slavery in the territories. Neither position suited the eight cotton states, who, following the lead of Jefferson Davis, withdrew from the Democratic Party and nominated their own presidential candidate, John C. Breckinridge, then the Vice-president. With the Democrats split, Lincoln won a sound electoral victory, (59%), but he received only 40% of the popular vote.

Vermont was the first state in the US to prohibit slavery, which it did in its constitution of 1791. In 1860 Vermont voted four to one for Lincoln over its native-son Douglas.

The Brandon Inn on the village green hosts a summer theater.

1.5   At the Pine Hill Cemetery (on the right), turn LEFT onto the unsigned road that runs northwest off US 7 past the Brandon Training School, which is visible on your left. (No sign may be in evidence at the cemetery, but it is the only cemetery in this vicinity.)

4.5   At the small sign (on the right) for Whiting, turn LEFT onto the

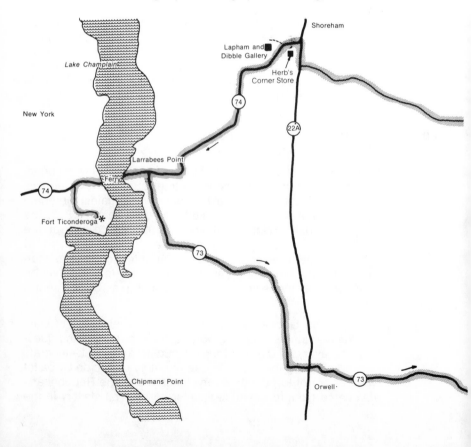

unsigned road toward Whiting.

8.5   At the Stop Sign in Whiting, go STRAIGHT across Route 30 onto the unsigned road toward Shoreham.

The Corner Cupboard on the left side of this intersection is the last place you can buy food until you reach Shoreham six miles away. In May, 1775, when Ethan Allen wanted to gather the Green Mountain Boys for their famous attack on Fort Ticonderoga, he dispatched Whiting blacksmith Samuel Beach as his messenger. The hearty Vermonter ran sixty-four miles in twenty-four hours to summon the backwoods clan for its sally across Lake Champlain.

14.5   At the Stop Sign, turn RIGHT onto Route 22A North.

15.0   At Herb's Corner Store (on the left) in Shoreham, turn LEFT onto Route 74 West.

In a quarter-mile on the right, is the outstanding Lapham and

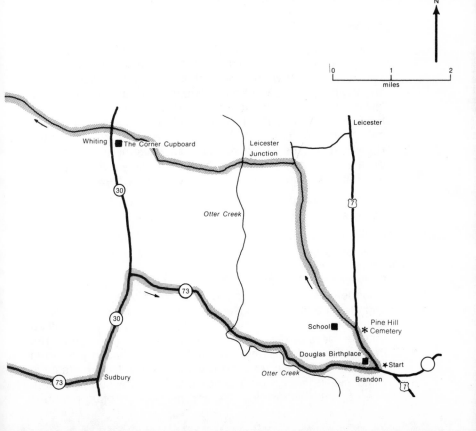

Dibble Gallery, which restores and sells fine American paintings and prints. It is definitely worth a visit. Shoreham sits at the heart of Addison County's prosperous apple-growing district and features a cooperative apple storage plant. Although more McIntosh are harvested than any other variety of apples, scores of kinds are grown in Addison County. From Shoreham, Route 74 descends to Larrabees Point on Lake Champlain.

20.0   At Larrabees Point, STOP to take the tiny Shorewell Ferry across Lake Champlain. After disembarking on the New York side, go STRAIGHT onto NY Route 74 West.

The Shorewell Ferry, which has been running for over two hundred years, operates from 8:00 a.m. to 6:00 p.m. The crossing takes only six minutes; consequently you should not have to wait more than fifteen. Cyclists and their bicycles are welcomed and charged about $2 round trip.

After the five Great Lakes, Champlain, covering 435 square miles, is the largest body of fresh water in the United States. Long and narrow, it begins 35 miles south of Larrabees Point and stretches northward 136 miles, the last 18 falling in Canada.

At its widest point, north of Burlington, the lake measures 15 miles, but most of it is much narrower. In winter it freezes to an average depth of twenty-two inches—enough to support cars and light trucks as well as ice fishermen. Champlain is one of few lakes in North America that flows northward, emptying into the Saint Lawrence River. A series of twelve locks near White-hall, New York, connects the lake at its southern end to the Hudson River. The swimming at Larrabees Point is not attractive, because this part of the lake has been badly polluted by the International Paper Company of Ticonderoga, New York.

The section of NY Route 74 which leads to Fort Ticonderoga is nearly all uphill.

20.5   At the sign for Fort Ticonderoga, turn LEFT and follow the mile-long driveway to the fort. After your visit, retrace your way back to the ferry and return to Vermont.

Between mid-May and mid-October visitors are welcome at Fort Ticonderoga from 8:00 a.m. to 5:00 p.m. Admission to the fort and its fine military museum is well worth the charge. A restaurant, gift shop, and large pleasant picnic area are located outside the stockade and are available without charge. The descendants of William Ferris Pell, who purchased the fort in ruins in 1820, have restored it magnificently. Now a National Historic Landmark, Fort Ticonderoga is still owned and managed by the Pell family. A fife and drum corps often performs outside the fort.

Militarily, the fort was key to Lake Champlain and served in turn the French, who built it, the British, the Revolutionary colonists, and the United States. Symbolically it has long been a monument to the audacity of Ethan Allen and his eighty-three Green Mountain Boys, who captured it from the sleeping British commander La Place in the morning darkness of May 10, 1775. Although their triumph was due to surprise rather than military force, it nevertheless greatly buoyed the spirits of the Revolutionary troops.

23.0 From the ferry landing at Larrabees Point, go STRAIGHT onto Route 74 East.

23.6 Turn RIGHT onto Route 73 East and follow its twists and turns through Orwell and Sudbury all the way back to Brandon.

This portion of the route—the sixteen miles from Larrabees Point to Otter Creek, three miles west of Brandon—makes the tour more demanding than moderate cycling. Route 73 mounts several hills, some steep and some long. These climbs are relieved by stretches of level riding and an occasional downhill run, but the ride is difficult because it also makes up in elevation the 450-foot difference between Brandon and Lake Champlain.

Orwell is the last place to buy food or drink until you reach Brandon, fourteen miles away. During the middle of the nineteenth century, Orwell became prosperous as a center of Vermont's vigorous wool industry. In the 1830s Merino sheep were the state's principal livestock, and most of the state was cleared for their pasture. Though sheep raising faded in Vermont after the Civil War, it is now enjoying a revival.

The Otter Creek makes poor swimming. At seventy-five miles the state's longest river, it flows lazily northward from Mount Tabor Town to Vergennes, where it empties into Lake Champlain. Along the way it gathers the runoff of thousands of acres of pastureland as well as some insufficiently treated industrial and residential waste.

43.6 At the Yield Sign, turn RIGHT onto US 7 South.

44.0 You are back in Brandon where the tour began.

Bicycle Repair Services
Bike & Ski Touring Center, 22 Main Street, Middlebury, VT (802-388-6666)
Green Mountain Schwinn Cyclery, 133 Strongs Avenue, Rutland, VT (802-775-0869)
Sports Peddler, 158 N Main Street (US 7), Rutland, VT (802-775-0101)
Vermont Bicycle Touring, Monkton Road, Bristol, VT (802-453-4811)

16

Middlebury–Vergennes

Easy terrain; 51 miles

Starting from the extraordinary college town and crafts center of Middlebury, this tour explores the historic Champlain Valley. Here in Addison County, flat and fertile farmlands nestling between the Green and Adirondack mountains provide some of the most panoramic views in Vermont. Fragrant apple orchards, rustling cornfields, and peaceful farms line the roads. Nearly level except for a mile and a half climb near the end, this tour provides an excellent opportunity to ride a Half-century in Vermont. (A Half-century is a bicycling standard established by the League of American Wheelmen whereby a cyclist must complete 50 miles in an elapsed, not riding, time of six hours or less. To ride a Century one must cover 100 miles in twelve hours; a Double Century, 200 in twenty-four.)

The route takes you through the campus of Middlebury College, along the shore of Lake Champlain, and near the sites of several important battles of the Revolution and War of 1812. The ride closes with a stop at the University of Vermont's Morgan Horse Farm and passage through one of only six remaining two-lane covered bridges in the United States. Start your ride at Jane and Frank Emanuel's gracious Middlebury Inn (1827), which treats bicyclists with great hospitality and serves a buffet dinner, generous enough to satisfy the appetites of the most ravenous riders.

0.0 From the Middlebury Inn follow Route 125 West toward Bridport.

Described in *A Walking History of Middlebury* by art historian Glenn M. Andres as a town that "has remained to a remarkable degree the village that the eighteenth and nineteenth centuries built," Middlebury is not merely of local architectural interest. According to Andres, its buildings document a "progression from frontier community to manufacturing center, to agricultural center, to local service center ... [and] can be taken as representative as well of almost every major style of American building from the colonial period onward."

At the center of town stand the magnificently restored John Warren House (1804), winner of a 1983 Honor Award from the Preservation Trust of Vermont, the Congregational Church

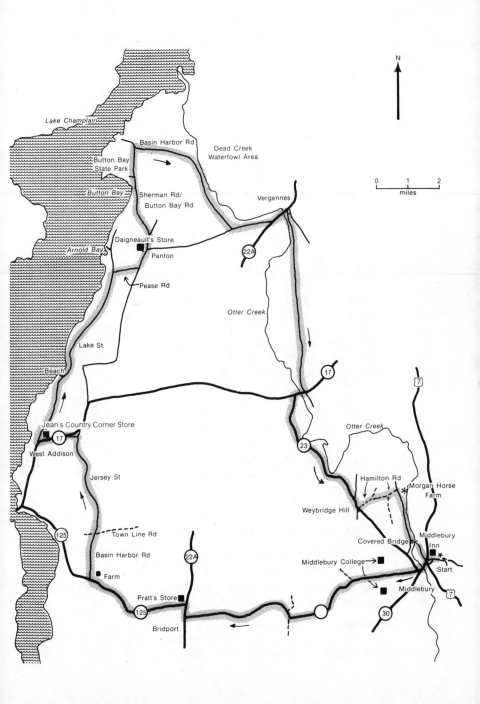

N

Lake Champlain

Basin Harbor Rd

Dead Creek
Waterfowl Area

Button Bay
State Park

Button Bay

Sherman Rd/
Button Bay Rd

Vergennes

0   1   2
miles

Daigneault's Store

Arnold Bay

Panton

22A

Pease Rd

Otter Creek

Lake St

Beach

17

7

Jean's Country Corner Store

Otter Creek

17

23

West Addison

Jersey St

Hamilton Rd

Morgan Horse
Farm

Weybridge Hill

Middlebury
Inn

Covered Bridge

125

Town Line Rd

Basin Harbor Rd

Start

Middlebury College →

22A

Farm

Middlebury

7

Pratt's Store

30

125

Bridport

(1806), the state's first craft center, and the Sheldon Museum, the oldest incorporated town museum in the nation. In an 1829 brick home, the museum displays an eclectic collection of artifacts of nineteenth-century New England life. It contains two handsomely appointed parlors, an old-fashioned country kitchen, a child's room complete with toys, dolls, and doll furniture, a country store, a tavern, extensive collections of pewter and Staffordshire, primitive portraits, and a library of old newspapers and other local historical records. The museum opens daily except Sundays and holidays from 10:00 a.m. to 5:00 p.m., June 1 to October 31. Admission is charged. Frog Hollow Craft Center is open year-round except Sundays from 10:00 a.m. to 5:00 p.m. A panel of judges has selected all the works on display, and all are for sale.

Many pleasant restaurants and specialty shops line the streets of the village. There are also several places from which you can select food for lunch, and you can eat better by carrying a picnic with you than by shopping along the way.

You pass through the campus of Middlebury College just as you leave the village. Founded in 1800 and coeducational since 1883, Middlebury is a highly selective, rather traditional liberal arts college with about two thousand students. During the summer, programs leading to advanced degrees in foreign languages are run at the Middlebury Campus. On Bread Loaf Mountain in nearby Ripton, the College offers a summer graduate program in English and American literature and a writers' conference, which Robert Frost helped found and taught for many years. The contemporary Christian A. Johnson Building, a hundred yards off the road on your right as you pass through the campus, displays paintings, sculptures, and graphics of students and professionals in its three-story open exhibition hall. The gallery is open to the public without charge daily from 1:00 p.m. to 5:00 p.m. The College provides free guided tours of its Middlebury campus from the Admissions Office in Emma Willard Hall (802-388-3711).

8.0   At the Stop Sign in Bridport, turn RIGHT to continue west on Route 125, which here runs concurrently with Route 22A North.

8.5   By Pratt's Store with Gulf gas pumps (on the left), turn LEFT to stay on Route 125 West.

12.0 By the farm with three silos (on the right), turn RIGHT onto Basin Harbor Road. You must look hard for this turn, for the street sign is on the left. In a mile and a half, after you cross Town Line Road,

Basin Harbor Road becomes Jersey Street.

16.5 At the intersection by the white West Addison Methodist Church (on the left), turn LEFT onto the unsigned road so you pass the front of the church on your right.

16.8 At the Stop Sign, turn LEFT onto Route 17 West. (There may not be a route marker at this intersection.)

17.8 At Jean's Country Corner Store (on the right) in West Addison, turn RIGHT onto Lake Street.
In just over a mile you have your first chance to swim in Lake Champlain. After passing a red house with a white fence on your left, turn left onto the Dead End road and ride a quarter-mile to the town beach. Though the beach is narrow and somewhat rocky, the water is clean and the swimming delightful. Lake Champlain covers 435 square miles, making it the sixth largest body of fresh water in the United States. It is 95 feet above sea level.

Over the next ten miles, as you glide through apple orchards and hayfields, the lake is often within sight. To your left across the water in New York State rise the Adirondack Mountains. And, provided the weather is clear, you can see the Green Mountains reaching across the eastern horizon, to your right. On the best of days you can see the five highest peaks in Vermont: from south to north, Killington (el. 4,235'), Abraham (el. 4,052'), Ellen (el. 4,083'), Camel's Hump (el. 4,083'), and Mansfield (4,393').

23.8 Turn RIGHT onto Pease Road.

24.6 At the T, turn LEFT onto Jersey Street.
Approach this turn cautiously. It comes suddenly when you are riding downhill, and sand often litters the road.

25.2 At the intersection in Panton, go STRAIGHT so you pass Daigneault's Store with Gulf gas pumps on your left.
Five miles from Panton, at the end of an unmarked road, lies Arnold Bay, which gained its name from a Revolutionary naval battle. In October, 1776, Benedict Arnold, who a year and a half earlier had accompanied Ethan Allen in the capture of Fort Ticonderoga, ingeniously outmaneuvered a larger British flotilla commanded by Admiral Guy Carleton. Carleton was sailing his powerful fleet south to attack Ticonderoga and the fortifications on Mount Independence near Orwell, when Arnold stealthily attacked. Although Arnold lost much of his fleet, he nevertheless achieved his main objective of obstructing Carleton's progress and thereby delaying the British advance southward. Before

they could assemble another offensive, the British were pre-
vented from sailing because the lake had frozen. Rather than
surrender even the battered ships he had used to block the
British fleet, Arnold ran them aground off Panton and set them
afire. The waterlogged hulls of these crafts are sometimes
visible when the lake is low, and cannonballs and other relics of
the encounter are still being uncovered.

25.7 At the fork, bear LEFT onto Sherman Road, which becomes Button
Bay Road.

In a mile and a half you reach Button Bay State Park, on the
lakeshore facing the Adirondack Mountains. The excellent
swimming and picnic facilities make an enticing rest stop.
Admission is charged, and the park is open from the Friday
before Memorial Day until mid-October, 10:00 a.m. to 9:00
p.m.

28.7 At the T, turn RIGHT onto Basin Harbor Road.

In about two miles you cross an exceptionally fine marsh in the
channel of Dead Creek. Here, on one thousand protected
acres, diverse plantlife provides excellent habitats for migrating
waterfowl, such as the Canada Goose, which passes through
late every fall and early each spring.

33.0 At the Stop Sign, turn LEFT onto the unsigned road.

34.3 At the Stop Sign, turn LEFT onto West Main Street, which is Route
22A North, to enter Vergennes.

Vergennes is the last place to buy food until the end of the tour.
You can eat at Vincent's Restaurant, which is an attractive place
in Stevens House, a recently remodeled 1793 building at the
southwest corner of the green. The green itself is an ideal place
to picnic, for it is well-kept and shaded and has its own drinking
fountain. You can buy an excellent fresh sandwich plus a wide
assortment of cheeses and other specialty items at the Owl's
Basket Gourmet Shop on Main Street, just around the corner from
Vincent's.

Vergennes is built around a falls on Otter Creek, just eight
navigable miles east of where that river empties into Lake
Champlain. During the War of 1812 the British planned a land
and naval offensive down Lake Champlain from Canada. In
order to meet the British attack, thirty-year-old Captain Thomas
Macdonough chose Vergennes as the place to winter (1813–14)
and strengthen his fleet. In the shipyards of Vergennes new
boats of Vermont timber were constructed in record time, and
177 tons of cannonballs were produced by the city's furnaces
and forges. Thus fortified, Macdonough soundly defeated the

British fleet of General Sir George Downie in a swift engagement that gave the United States undisputed control of the lake and saved Vermont from British occupation. This victory helped redeem Vermont's reputation for the widespread private smuggling of beef into Canada, where, according to General George Izard of the American army, it had been saving British forces from starvation.

34.8 Beside Eris Portraits (on the right), turn RIGHT onto the unsigned road.

34.9 At the Stop Sign, go STRAIGHT across the intersection to continue south on the unsigned road from Vergennes.

41.0 At the Stop Sign, turn RIGHT onto Route 17 West. (There may be no

Along the shore of Lake Champlain near West Addison; the Adirondacks are at the horizon.

route marker at this intersection.)

41.4 Turn LEFT onto Route 23 South.

In about three miles the tour's only difficult hill begins its mile-and-a-half climb into Weybridge Hill.

46.4 At Weybridge Hill, follow Route 23 through the intersection and then, immediately after passing the red brick Weybridge Congregational Church (on the left), turn LEFT onto Hamilton Road, which is unpaved. Do not turn onto either Cave Road or Sheep Farm Road, both of which are unpaved and intersect Hamilton Road. Hamilton Road can be soft, and it may be safer to walk in places.

47.8 At the T, turn RIGHT onto the paved, unsigned road.

In a half-mile the entrance to the Morgan Horse Farm, a National Historic Site, is on your left. Centered around a handsome 1878 barn and run by the University of Vermont, the farm raises prizewinning Morgans. The Morgan, Vermont's state animal, is the oldest breed of light horse developed in America, its lineage dating to 1790. Though not a large horse, it possesses a wonderful variety of abilities and can be trained for plowing, cutting cattle, dressage, jumping, pleasure riding, show, police work, driving carts, and trotting. Morgans take their name from Justin Morgan, a singing teacher and composer of some note, who brought his colt Figure here from Massachusetts nearly two hundred years ago. Colonel Joseph Battell of Middlebury established the farm, gave it to the United States in 1906, and compiled the original Morgan registry. His love for horses may have grown from his hatred of automobiles. While publisher of the Middlebury *Register*, Battell wrote a column entitled "Chamber of Horrors," where he dramatically described automobile accidents. The farm offers guided tours of its grounds and stables and a slide show about Morgans daily from 8:00 a.m. to 4:00 p.m., May 1 to November 1. There is a charge for the tour but no admission fee to the grounds and main barn.

49.3 At the tiny traffic island, bear LEFT and walk or ride slowly and very carefully through the covered bridge; it is dark and slippery.

Reaching 179 feet across Otter Creek, the recently renovated Pulpmill covered bridge (c. 1820) is the oldest in the state and one of only two double-lane covered bridges in Vermont, the other being at the Shelburne Museum and not open to traffic.

49.9 At the Stop Sign, 200 yards beyond Champlain Valley Equipment and Ford Tractors (on the left), turn LEFT and ride through the underpass.

50.0 Opposite Greg's Meat Market (on the left), turn RIGHT onto Seymour Street. (There may not be a sign at this intersection.)

50.5 At the Stop Sign, you are beside Middlebury's Congregational Church (1806), the magnificent product of Connecticut-born Lavius Fillmore, who also built the First Congregational Church in Bennington. The Middlebury Inn is a hundred yards away to your left.

Bicycle Repair Services
Bike & Ski Touring Center, 22 Main Street, Middlebury, VT (802-388-6666)
Vermont Bicycle Touring, Monkton Road, Bristol, VT (802-453-4811)

17

Bristol–Starksboro

Easy–to–moderate terrain; 24 miles

This tour nestles in the Champlain Valley, some of the most prosperous farmland in the northeast. Though there are a few short, steep climbs, the terrain is relatively flat. The farms are pleasingly small, and the foothills of the Green Mountains scallop the horizon. Though dairy farming predominates, apples, honey, maple syrup, wool, lamb, and beef are also raised here. In August roadside stands overflow with ripe, colorful vegetables.

The Champlain Valley was created during the Pleistocene Glacial Age. A huge sheet of ice crept southward from Labrador, rearranging rocks and soil, sculpting the mountains, and widening the valley. Waters from the melting ice and invading sea then flooded the valley hundreds of feet deep. Marine fossils are still being discovered far above sea level.

Bristol is a pleasant, unpretentious, pretty village. Consider starting your day with breakfast at the Kountry Kupboard at 24 Main Street. The homemade bread is excellent, either as French toast with maple syrup or with eggs. The tour starts in the center of Bristol.

0.0 At the Traffic Light at the intersection of Main, West, and North Streets—with the village green on your left—turn LEFT onto North Street. The sign for North Street is on your left on the edge of the green a tenth-mile beyond the traffic light.

In one and three-quarters miles you reach the headquarters of Vermont Bicycle Touring (VBT) in a pale yellow barn and farmhouse (1848) on the right. VBT, which I founded in 1972, is the oldest and largest firm in America offering country inn bicycling vacations. Please come in, if we can be of help to you. Across from VBT is the Winona Recreation Area (802-453-3439), which rents tent and trailer camping sites from May 1 to October 15.

2.1 Follow the main road—from here northward known as Monkton Road, though it is unsigned—as it curves to the RIGHT. Thereafter, follow the main road straight; do not turn onto the sideroads.

In a mile and three-quarters on the right is an unpaved road which leads to Bristol Pond, good for northern pike and largemouth bass. A large variety of Indian relics has been uncovered along the shores.

Three miles beyond the turn-off to the pond, Monkton Road tips slightly upward. The slope increases gradually for a mile and then suddenly turns steep into what feels like a wall but is only four-tenths mile long.

9.3 At the intersection in Monkton Ridge, go STRAIGHT but ride only a hundred yards to the first road on your right. There, bear RIGHT onto the unsigned road that goes downhill so you pass the Russell Memorial Library, housed in a small white clapboard building, on your right.

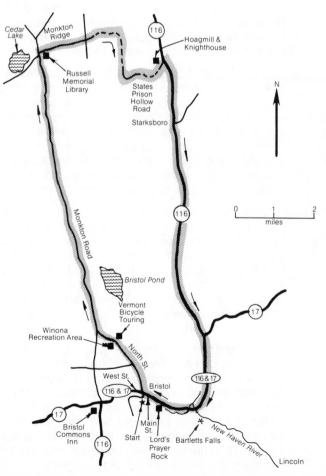

Before heading eastward out of town, consider riding through this one-street village to see the Adirondacks sweeping across the western horizon and the top of Camel's Hump (el. 4,083'), peeking over the Green Mountains in the east. You can buy a snack and creemee at the Monkton General Store.

From Monkton Ridge the road runs downhill for a mile and a half.

10.7 At the crossroad, go STRAIGHT onto the unsigned road, which becomes unpaved in a tenth-mile. The name of this road is States Prison Hollow, but it is unsigned here, and there is no prison nearby.

The road rolls steeply uphill for a half-mile and then downhill for a half-mile. It stays unpaved for one and a half miles. Then for three-quarters of a mile it is paved—to the bottom of a short, moderately steep hill, where the road again becomes unpaved. From the bottom you climb a half-mile to the top, where the surface becomes paved once again.

Just before the next turn, you pass a striking homestead of finely restored buildings on the left. The principal structures, both listed in the National Register of Historic Places, are the Hoag stone mill (1799) and the Knight house (1831). The first, originally a gristmill and later as a sawmill, remained in operation until the depression of the 1930s. Its walls are three feet thick. The buildings are now a private home. In 1969 they were the subject of a feature story in *Vermont Life*.

14.0 At the Stop Sign, turn RIGHT onto Route 116 South, which is unsigned here, and follow it all the way back to Bristol.

For the first three-quarters of a mile you ride gradually uphill. Then an easy half-mile carries you into Starksboro, where a solitary general store stands on the right. From the store you climb a difficult half-mile to the height of the land, and thereafter the cycling is easy all the way to Bristol. Starksboro was named for the American Revolutionary General John Stark, hero at the battles of Bunker Hill and Bennington.

In eight and three-quarters miles, just before Route 116 curves right to cross a small bridge, you reach on your left a paved road that runs uphill to Lincoln and Warren. If you take that road you can treat yourself to the joy of an old-fashioned swimming hole. The New Haven River tumbles alongside the road through a series of marvelous cascades and waterfalls. The most popular place to swim is at the base of Bartletts Falls, just a third-mile off Route 116 at the top of the first rise. If you ride further, you can usually find a beautiful spot all to yourself.

Continuing southward on Route 116, you reach the stolid Lord's Prayer Rock (1891) in a mile on your left. Here, thanks to the generosity and righteousness of a Buffalo, New York, physician, Joseph Greene, who spent his boyhood in Bristol, the Lord's Prayer is inscribed on the face of an enormous boulder. Apparently Greene thought the profane language of teamsters, urging their horses along Bristol's muddy roads a century ago, might be improved by this immense invocation. There's no evidence that the good doctor's efforts went unheeded, but, although the roads are now paved, the hillsides of Bristol still occasionally ring with the blasphemous exclamations of travelers. Some claim even bicyclists are not immune to the temptation!

24.2 At the Traffic Light, you are again beside the green on Main Street in Bristol.

Dining here is a treat. Mary's Restaurant at 11 Main Street has been a favorite of mine for years. It serves a delectable variety of carefully prepared continental dinners as well as lunch and Sunday brunch; it also has a fine beer and wine list. Rosemarie's Restaurant at the Bristol Commons Inn, a mile south of the village on routes 116 and 17, opened in 1983 and is already widely known for its excellent and very extensive Italian menu.

Bristol also features an interesting antique shop, called King's Barn Annex, at 19 Main Street. And, if you're in town on Wednesday evening around 8:00 between late May and early September, you can hear a free concert, performed by a citizens' band in the cupola on the green.

Bicycle Repair Services
Bike and Ski Touring Center, 22 Main Street, Middlebury, VT (802-388-6666)
Earl's Schwinn Cyclery, 142 Dorset Street, South Burlington, VT (802-864-9197 & 864-6190)
The Outfitters, Ethan Allen Shopping Center, Burlington, VT (802-863-1257)
Pagocycle, 227 Main Street, Burlington, VT (802-864-6878)
The Ski Rack Bike Shop, 81 Main Street, Burlington, VT (802-658-3313)
Vermont Bicycle Touring, Monkton Road, Bristol, VT 05443 (802-453-4811)

Northwestern Vermont

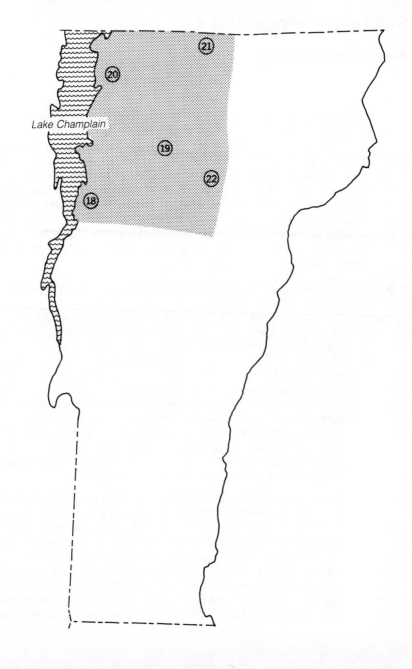

18

Shelburne–Hinesburg

Easy terrain; 18.5 miles

This tour offers an opportunity to combine a visit to one of the nation's greatest collections of American folk art with a short, delightfully pastoral ride in the Champlain Valley. Being open and mostly flat, the terrain not only affords panoramic views but makes the bicycling easy. Although nearly one-quarter of Vermont's 500,000 residents live within twenty-five miles of here, this route uses roads with little traffic. Shelburne, where the tour begins, has rightly acquired nationwide fame for its extraordinary museum. The village itself, shaded by sugar maples and elms, boasts a variety of charming shops selling antiques, artworks, woodenware, crafts, foods, and country kitchenware.

0.0 From the blinker on US 7 in Shelburne, follow Mt. Philo Road south so you pass the Shelburne Country Store on your left.

If you have a half-day either before you begin cycling or afterwards, try to spend it at the Shelburne Museum. Nowhere in Vermont and few places in the United States display a finer or more varied collection of Americana. Founded in 1947 by Electra Havemeyer Webb, the Shelburne Museum consists of thirty-five buildings and the *S.S. Ticonderoga*, the last vertical beam passenger and freight sidewheeler remaining intact in this country. Spread over one hundred beautifully groomed and gardened acres on the west side of US 7, a quarter-mile south of the light at Mt. Philo Road, the museum is open daily from mid–May to mid–October, 9:00 a.m. to 5:00 p.m. Admission is charged to everyone but Vermont teachers who are admitted free.

The museum reflects the eclectic taste of its founder, who began collecting American craft and folk art before its artistic merit was widely recognized. Many of the buildings are important historical artifacts themselves and were dismantled and moved to Shelburne piece by piece. Four examples are: Prentis House (1733, Hadley, Massachusetts), a salt-box outfitted with seventeenth- and eighteenth-century furniture, delftware, and stumpwork embroidery; the Shelburne Railroad Station (1890), an example of Victorian architecture now filled with railroading memorabilia and beside which are parked a ten-wheel steam locomotive and an opulent private railroad car; a stagecoach inn (c. 1783, from nearby Charlotte), now housing sculptured folk art, including many cigar store Indians, trade signs, circus figures, and weathervanes; and Dorset House (c. 1840, East Dorset, Vermont) where Audubon prints, Joel Barber watercolors, and one thousand decoys are displayed. Among many other things, the museum contains a 525-foot-long scale model of a circus parade and two galleries of important paintings. The Webb Gallery features American primitive and academic works by Edward Hicks, Erastus Salisbury Field, Andrew Wyeth, Winslow Homer, and Albert Bierstadt among others. At the Electra Havemeyer Webb Building, in Georgian paneled rooms removed from the magnificent New York apartment of Mrs. Webb's in-laws, hang two paintings by Rembrandt and several by Monet as well as works of Manet, Whistler,

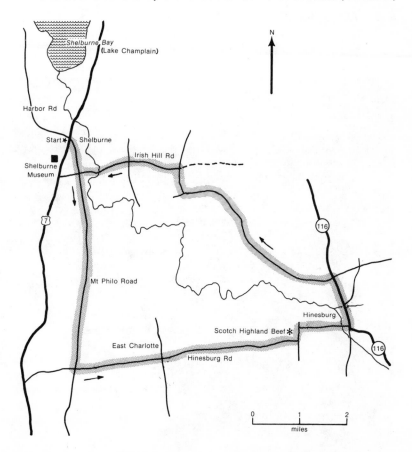

Goya, Mary Cassatt, and Degas. The museum also has a cafeteria and picnic area.

Should you wish to buy food to carry while you are bicycling, stop by Harrington's, which sells its own smoked meats and Vermont cheeses, or the Shelburne Country Store. Both are located near the intersection of Mt. Philo Road and US 7.

0.7   At the Stop Sign, go STRAIGHT across the intersection and ride south on Mt. Philo Road.

From Mt. Philo Road, if the day is clear, you can make out the distinctive shape of Camel's Hump (el. 4,083′), Vermont's fourth tallest mountain, and also Mount Mansfield (el. 4,393′), the tallest. Both rise in the east to your left. To your right you can glimpse the Adirondack Mountains at one or two points if you look carefully.

4.6   At the Stop Sign, turn LEFT onto Hinesburg Road.

During the next six miles the road rolls over several small hills, providing roughly equal amounts of short climbs and descents.

6.4 At the blinker in East Charlotte, go STRAIGHT toward Hinesburg.
In about three and a half miles, as you turn a ninety-degree curve
to the left, you may notice some peculiar cattle grazing in a small
pasture by the road. These animals with reddish brown hair and
long horns that can measure three feet in width are Scotch High-
land Beef cattle.

10.8 At the Stop Sign in Hinesburg, turn LEFT onto Route 116 North toward
Richmond.
Hinesburg is the last place you can buy food. There are good
grocery stores, but I enjoy most Arthur's Deli in the Hinesburg
Village Center. From this Stop Sign, ride just a tenth mile north on
Route 116 and then turn right toward Lake Iroquois and Richmond. You will find Arthur's Deli in 250 yards on the right. Arthur,
an emigrant New Yorker and ex-potter of note, now makes homemade soups, salads, sandwiches, and pastries. His deli is open
seven days a week.

11.8 At the blinker, turn LEFT onto the unsigned road away from Champlain
Valley Union High School.
Between 2:30 p.m. and 4:00 p.m. on school days, traffic between
here and Shelburne can be bothersome.

15.8 At the ninety-degree bend in the road, follow the main road to the
RIGHT.

16.3 At the Stop Sign, turn LEFT onto Irish Hill Road.

17.3 At the crossroad, go STRAIGHT to continue on Irish Hill Road.

18.0 At the Stop Sign, turn RIGHT onto Mt. Philo Road.

18.5 You are now back in Shelburne where you began.
If you would like to go swimming, go straight at the blinker across
US 7 onto Harbor Road. Then follow Harbor Road four miles to
Shelburne Point on Lake Champlain, where you can swim off the
rocks. Just after crossing US 7 you pass the Shelburne Craft
School Shop, which sells weavings, woodwork, pottery, stained
glass, graphics, and jewelry made by its students and staff.

Bicycle Repair Services
Adams Bicycle Services (house calls only), Williston, VT (802-879-1192)
Earl's Schwinn Cyclery, 142 Dorset Street, South Burlington, VT (802-864-9197
& 864-6190)
Pagocycle, 227 Main Street, Burlington, VT (802-864-6878)
The Outfitters, Ethan Allen Shopping Center, Burlington, VT (802-863-1257)
The Ski Rack Bike Shop, 81 Main Street, Burlington, VT (802-658-3313)
Vermont Bicycle Touring, Monkton Road, Bristol, VT (802-453-4811)

19

Cambridge–Underhill Center

Moderate terrain; 24 miles

From the spacious, orderly old village of Cambridge, this tour etches a circle through farmlands at the base of Vermont's highest mountain. Few roads in the state make a more intimate connection with a mountain than aptly named Pleasant Valley Road makes with the massive profile of Mount Mansfield. It leads you along the western flank of the mountain just far enough away to appreciate the mountain's size and yet close enough to see in detail the rocks and vegetation on its slopes. Along the way you can also visit one of Vermont's most established potters and an experimental farm where scientists are studying the mysterious workings of sugar maples. The tour starts from Cambridge so you may ride on Route 15 as early in the day as possible. Route 15 draws more traffic than bicyclists normally need encounter in Vermont, but to ride it for ten miles in order to follow Pleasant Valley Road for fourteen is a good bargain.

0.0   Leave Cambridge by riding west on Route 15.

Cambridge was settled in 1783 during that extraordinary time when Vermont was an independent nation, 1777–91. The unusually wide thoroughfare in the center of the village was built to enable the local militia to hold their musters without interfering with traffic. Cambridge lies on a broad intervale along the Lamoille River, one of the few Vermont rivers canoeable in both spring and summer. Due to the ridge of mountains running like a spine through the center of the state, rivers in Vermont generally flow down the eastern slope of the mountains into the Connecticut River or down the western slope into Lake Champlain. However the Lamoille, along with the Winooski and Missisquoi, are exceptions; rising in the east, they flow westward *through* the mountains to Lake Champlain. These rivers apparently anteceded the formation of the Green Mountains and when the latter rose were able to carve themselves valleys rapidly enough to maintain their courses. From Cambridge upstream to Johnson the Lamoille offers especially good cover for brown trout.

An interesting small botanical area sits in a ravine behind the

Cambridge cemetery. Called the Cambridge Pine Woods after a stand of large white pine whose trunks measure as much as forty-eight inches in diameter, the Woods also contain hemlocks, sugar maples, red oaks, and herbs. At the eastern end of the village, near where Route 15 curves sharply over the Lamoille River, you can find the Gates Farm covered bridge. Built in 1897 and moved to its present site in 1951, its Burr Arch spans sixty feet.

0.7   At the intersection of Routes 15 and 104, turn LEFT to continue west on Route 15.

As soon as you make the turn, you start up a gentle to moderate hill a mile and a half long. Then, after a flat half-mile, the road tips downward into a gradual two-and-a-half-mile descent. As the descent fades away, the Scatchard Stoneware Workshop comes into view on your right. George Scatchard and his friends make stoneware lamps here. The workshop is open between 9:00 a.m. and 5:00 p.m., Monday through Saturday and some-

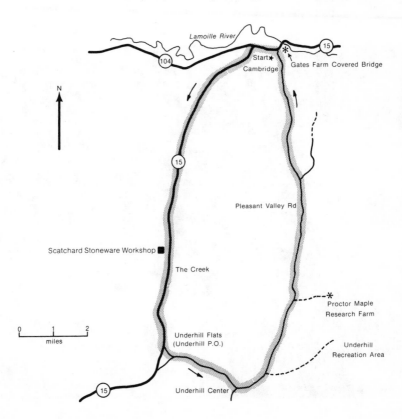

times on Sunday. Past Scatchard's, Route 15 rolls uphill for a half-mile, downhill for three-quarters, and then uphill for another half-mile. From Scatchard's to Underhill Flats, look for wildlife, for you are riding near a thousand-acre preserve called The Creek, where beavers have dammed a meandering stream, creating a series of ponds and extensive marshlands.

10.4 At the triangle (on the left) in Underhill Flats (Underhill P.O.), turn LEFT off Route 15 toward Underhill Center.
Settled in 1786, Underhill sits under the wing of Mount Mansfield (el. 4,393'), Vermont's highest mountain. According to most accounts the town takes its name from its location. According to some sources, Underhill was named for two brothers who settled the town and originally owned much of its land. Within two hundred yards you come to Jacobs IGA Market on your right. You can find ample lunch supplies there to carry to one of the beautiful spots on Pleasant Valley Road for a picnic.

10.8 At the T, turn LEFT onto Pleasant Valley Road. (There is no street sign at this intersection.)

For the next two and three-quarter miles you follow the Browns River into the small village of Underhill Center. You can buy more food there at the K & T Country Store on the left. St. Thomas Catholic Church, which dominates the center of the village, contains several fine stained-glass windows. The Underhill Town Hall occupies the former Old White Church, built in 1850.

One mile north of the village you pass the entrance to the Underhill Recreation Area. Though this park is beautifully situated, it offers no swimming and is difficult to reach. The four-mile ride to get there goes up a precipitous grade on an unpaved road and is enjoyable only if you are seeking that sort of challenge.

Immediately beyond the entrance to the recreation area, you start a strenuous climb of a mile and a quarter. Then along a level half-mile you pass the driveway to the University of Vermont's Proctor Maple Research Farm. Throughout the year researchers from the Vermont Agricultural Experiment Station investigate ways to facilitate and improve the making of maple sugar products. During the sugaring season, which usually comes in March, sap is gathered and boiled into syrup on the farm. Visitors are welcome from 9:00 a.m. to 3:00 p.m., Monday through Friday, year-round. The mile-long, unpaved driveway into the farm runs mostly uphill.

You reach the height-of-land a mile beyond the entrance to the Maple Research Farm. There you can picnic in the shade of a sugar maple and look across rolling meadows to Mount Mansfield. The rest of the way back to Cambridge, seven and three-quarter miles away, goes downhill about half the time.

20.2 At the fork in Pleasant Valley, which consists only of this intersection, bear LEFT toward Cambridge.

24.0 At the Stop Sign, you are facing Route 15 back in Cambridge where the tour began.

Bicycle Repair Services

Adams Bicycle Services (house calls only), Williston, VT (802-879-1192)

Demers Repair Inc., 81 South Main Street, Barre, VT (802-476-7712)

Earl's Schwinn Cyclery, 142 Dorset Street, South Burlington, VT (802-864-9197 and 864-6190)

Onion River Sports, 20 Langdon Street, Montpelier, VT (802-229-9409)

Pagocycle, 227 Main Street, Burlington, VT (802-864-6878)

The Outfitters, Essex Junction Shopping Center, Essex Junction, VT (802-879-7826)

The Ski Rack Bike Shop, 81 Main Street, Burlington, VT (802-658-3313)

20
St. Albans—Swanton

Easy terrain; 25 miles

From St. Albans this tour follows a route without hills along the Missisquoi River and northern shore of Lake Champlain. Henry Ward Beecher thought St. Albans sat "in the midst of a greater variety of scenic beauty than any other [place] I can remember in America." That may still be largely true, but many changes have occurred in the hundred years since Beecher was writing. Trees have died or been removed to make way for construction, and houses have risen along the banks of the lake and river; so prepare yourself to feel occasionally frustrated by what humankind has done to this extraordinary region.

Nevertheless, the tour offers many beautiful views, a fine place to swim, and exceptional opportunities to see waterfowl and other migrating birds. Being short as well as level, it allows lots of time for exploration. It also lends itself to cycling early and late in the season, for Lake Champlain tempers the climate, hastening spring and stalling winter. With no leaves on the trees the views are better, and with fewer vacationers about, the roads are nearly yours alone. Moreover, if you do the tour in April, you can combine it with a visit to the Vermont Maple Sugar Festival in St. Albans. That is a joyous occasion, with sugar on snow, lumberjack contests, square dances, pancake breakfasts, a fiddling contest, and much more. (For scheduling information, contact the Chamber of Commerce, 78 North Main Street, St. Albans, VT 05478 (802-524-2444).

0.0 From Taylor Park, the large green in the center of St. Albans, follow US 7 (North Main Street) North out of town.

St. Albans has witnessed some curious events because of its proximity to Canada. Before the railroad reached St. Albans, potash was the city's only saleable product, and Montreal its only market. But in 1807 the passage of Thomas Jefferson's Embargo Act forbade trade with all foreign nations, and the good folk of St. Albans became deeply involved in smuggling One St. Albans merchant hired a craft, named *Black Snake*, to run potash into Canada. His business thrived for several months until the border patrol discovered *Black Snake* and chased it

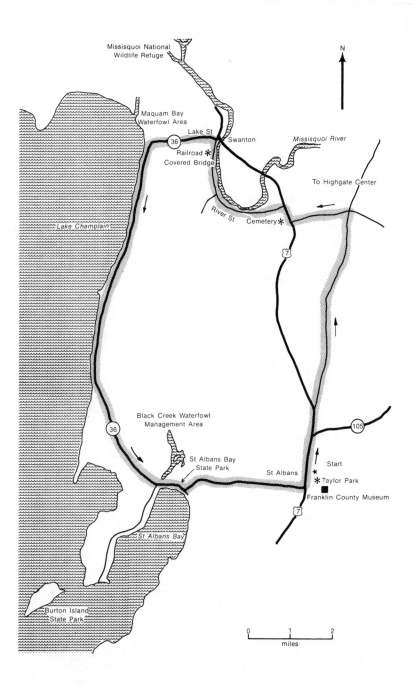

Missisquoi National
Wildlife Refuge

N

Maquam Bay
Waterfowl Area

Lake St

36

Swanton

Missisquoi River

Railroad ✳
Covered Bridge

To Highgate Center

River St

Cemetery ✳

Lake Champlain

7

Black Creek Waterfowl
Management Area

36

105

St Albans Bay
State Park

St Albans

Start

St Albans Bay

✳ Taylor Park
■
Franklin County Museum

7

Burton Island
State Park

0   1   2
miles

down Lake Champlain. At Burlington a bloody battle ensued with the smugglers killing three federal officers and wounding several others before losing their craft. Opposition to the Embargo Act ran so deeply in Vermont, as it did throughout New England, that only one of the smugglers was executed. The others were imprisoned and subsequently pardoned.

With the completion of the railroad in 1850, prosperity came to St. Albans. Ironically that prosperity indirectly caused the most memorable day in St. Albans's history. At three o'clock in the afternoon of October 19, 1864, twenty-two rebel soldiers seeking funds for the Confederacy converged on St. Albans. Simultaneously they entered all the banks, unburdened them of over $200,000, killed one man, and wounded several others. They then hustled their booty across the border to Canada, burning the Sheldon covered bridge behind them. Thus did St. Albans become the site of the Civil War's northernmost engagement, if that it can be called. The Franklin-Lamoille Bank at 8 North Main Street has photomurals of the raid and helped publish a pamphlet about it in 1971.

Other mementos of the raid, including some of the stolen currency and a broadside entitled "Orleans County Awake, Rebels in Vermont!", are exhibited at the Franklin County Museum, which faces the eastern edge of Taylor Park. The museum's large and diverse collection also contains two interesting medical exhibits. One consists of the memorabilia of William Beaumont, a surgeon who studied in St. Albans from 1810 to 1812 and contributed greatly to medical research by reporting on the digestive system of a patient who had a permanent hole in his stomach from a gunshot wound. The other exhibit contains the furnishings from Dr. George Russell's Arlington, Vermont, office, made famous by Norman Rockwell in his painting, "The Family Doctor," which appeared on a 1947 cover of *The Saturday Evening Post*.

The museum also contains period costumes, railroad memorabilia, old farm implements, and a maple sugaring exhibit. The museum is open 2:00 to 5:00 p.m. Tuesday through Saturday, during July and August. Admission is free; contributions appreciated.

On your way out of St. Albans, you pass two especially fine old houses: the Stranahan House (c. 1850) at 149 North Main and the city's oldest building, the Hoyt House, formerly a tavern built in 1793, at 255 North Main Street. Other buildings worth seeing are the Houghton House, built in 1801 and now a national historic site and realtor's office, at 86 South Main Street, and the

Congregational Church and the Franklin County Court House, both of which face Taylor Park near the museum. Finally, you might stop by the Vermont Information Center at 128 North Main Street to inquire whether any special events are taking place while you are in the area.

Bicycling on US 7 requires your complete attention. Not only is the traffic usually heavy, but vehicles may be backing out of diagonal parking spaces, stopping suddenly, turning onto the road, and turning off it without signaling properly.

2.1 Bear RIGHT off US 7 onto the road toward Highgate Center and Interstate 89.

Just before reaching the next turn, if the weather is clear, you can see Jay Peak (el. 3,861') off to your right.

6.4 At the crossroad, turn LEFT onto the unsigned road.

7.5 At the Stop Sign, turn RIGHT onto US 7 North.

7.8 Two-tenths mile beyond the cemetery (on the left), turn LEFT off US 7 onto the unsigned road. (At its western end in Swanton, this road is called River Street.)

Over the next two miles you follow the Missisquoi River toward Lake Champlain. Missisquoi means "much grass" and "many waterfowl," which comes as no surprise once you see the river. The Missisquoi National Wildlife Refuge covers 4,792 acres of marshland less than five miles away so you might see some interesting birds. Over 180 species—including osprey, great horned owl, bald eagle, and great blue heron—have been sited in the refuge.

9.8 At the Stop Sign, turn RIGHT onto the unsigned road so you continue along the Missisquoi River. Do not ride across the railroad tracks.

A quarter-mile before your next turn, you pass the Swanton Railroad covered bridge. Built in 1898, the three spans of this bridge measure 369 feet, making it the longest railroad covered bridge still standing in Vermont.

10.8 On the outskirts of Swanton, turn LEFT onto Lake Street, which is Route 36 South. (You can easily miss this turn, and, if you do, you will pass an antique shop on the right and then reach a Stop Sign.)

The antique shop merits a look. If the door is locked, you can call the owner Gordon Winters at 802-868-3322 or find him at the Swanton Lumber Company, one block straight ahead from the Stop Sign. Winters sells an interesting assortment of furniture, clocks, and other collectibles; in 1977 I bought a nineteenth-century wooden-wheel, safety bicycle from him.

Like St. Albans, Swanton is no stranger to smuggling. The bootleggers of the Roaring Twenties who drove Canadian whiskey into Vermont here were the spiritual descendents of Vermont farmers who drove cattle into Canada to sell them to the starving British soldiers during the War of 1812.

Each year near the end of July, Swanton produces a Summer Festival that includes art and craft exhibits, band concerts, barbershop quartet singing, a lumberjack roundup, a chicken barbecue, a parade, and a fairway with rides and concessions. For details and a schedule, contact the Swanton Chamber of Commerce, Box 182, Swanton, VT 05488 (802-868-7200).

A mile and three-quarters after turning onto Route 36, you pass the Maquam Bay Waterfowl Area, reach Lake Champlain, and begin a six-mile ride along its shoreline. The sixth largest body of fresh water in the United States, Lake Champlain covers 435 square miles and stretches 118 miles down Vermont's western border. In the winter the lake freezes to a depth of nearly two feet and supports a multitude of fishing shanties. Although private homes, cottages, and trees occasionally obstruct your view, you can often see across the lake to the Adirondack Mountains. A mile and a quarter after the road pulls away from the lakeshore, Camel's Hump (el. 4,083'), Vermont's fourth highest peak, looms into view far in the southeast. Once you know its name, you can always identify it.

21.2 At the rotary where the road to Burton Island State Park branches off Route 36 to the right, go STRAIGHT to stay on Route 36 South and follow it across the iron bridge.

Burton Island offers the best swimming and picnicking on the tour as well as good fishing. To reach the park, turn right here and ride three and a half miles along the shoreline of St. Albans Bay to Lake Champlain. From there you must take a boat, for which there is a charge, and leave your bicycle on the mainland. You can arrange to have a boat meet you by calling 802-524-6353, but you may find a boat there when you arrive anyway. The 253-acre island remains undeveloped except the sites set aside for camping, swimming, and picnicking. Admission is charged.

21.9 The entrance to St. Albans Bay State Park is on your right.

This park has a snack bar but poor swimming because the waters of St. Albans Bay are polluted and nurture weeds and algae. Admission is charged.

22.1 At Booth's Market (with Arco gas pumps on the left), turn LEFT to follow Route 36 East.

In three miles, just as you reenter St. Albans, you pass some of the grand railroad architecture for which the city is rightly known. Most of the buildings seem neglected, but the thought and aesthetic considerations which went into their design are clearly evident.

25.0   At the traffic light, you are facing Taylor Park where the tour began.

Bicycle Repair Services

Adams Bicycle Services (house calls only), Williston, VT (802-879-1192)

Earl's Schwinn Cyclery, 142 Dorset Street, South Burlington, VT (802-864-9197 & 864-6190)

Endurance Sports, 82 North Main Street, St. Albans, VT (802-524-4685)

Jason's Sport, 108 Lake Street, St. Albans, VT (802-524-3312)

Pagocycle, 227 Main Street, Burlington, VT (802-864-6878)

The Outfitters, Essex Junction Shopping Center, Essex Junction, VT (802-879-7826)

The Ski Rack Bike Shop, 81 Main Street, Burlington, VT (802-658-3313)

21
Enosburg Falls–Richford

Moderate–to–difficult terrain; 33 miles

Beginning in the town of Enosburg Falls, this tour offers my favorite bicycling along the Vermont–Quebec border. Few places in the United States have such extraordinary beauty and roads as free of traffic as northwestern Vermont. The tour winds through rolling farmlands fringed by thousands of sugar maples and bounded by the mountains. Falling at the northern end of the Green Mountain chain, the route is relatively hilly, though it never crosses a mountain pass, and so warrants a moderate–to–difficult rating. But the undulations of the terrain provide several superb downhill runs and many sweeping views of the mountains. Following the Missisquoi and Trout rivers along its final and easiest third, the tour also passes three old covered bridges.

0.0 From the Enosburg Falls green follow Route 108 North toward West Berkshire

Before leaving town, you might want to get some food to carry along, since there are no groceries or restaurants until Richford, fourteen miles away.

One of a few towns that the Republic of Vermont chartered during its fourteen years as an independent nation (1777–91), Enosburg Falls is now best known for maple syrup and the springtime Vermont Dairy Festival. Held just outside the village on the first Saturday of June, the Festival features a parade, livestock shows, horse pulling contests, barbecues, and lots of country fiddling and square dancing. Though it draws considerable traffic to the area, only Route 105 is usually affected. It would be fun to combine an early springtime ride with a visit to the Dairy Festival.

In the early nineteenth century an Enosburg settler named Isaac Farrar developed wooden spouts for tapping sugar maple trees. Though the effectiveness of the spouts quickly led to their widespread use, Farrar's neighbors nevertheless accused him of "scientific farming," which then was not the vogue that it has become. Later in the nineteenth century Enosburg Falls acquired a substantial reputation as the home of panaceas and patent medicines, "guaranteed" to cure nearly every ill of man or beast. At least four local entrepreneurs amassed fortunes with their cures, and some people say that descendants of the original manufacturers still pursue the business.

Route 108 goes gently uphill much of the way to West Berkshire. About two and a half miles north of Enosburg Falls, stop to take a look at the view behind you. To the east stands Jay Peak (el. 3,861'), readily identifiable by its cone-shaped top on which a ski life now perches. Mount Mansfield, at 4,393' the state's tallest summit, rises directly behind you in the south.

6.0   At the Stop Sign in West Berkshire, turn RIGHT off Route 108 onto the unnumbered road toward Berkshire. (Just after making this turn, you pass an Arco station on your left.)

Should you want to go into Canada, you can get there easily by continuing north two miles further on Route 108. You should carry at least a driver's license as identification, if you actually cross the border. About twelve miles northwest of West Berkshire at Eccles Hill in Quebec, the Fenians, a secret Irish brotherhood organized in the 1850s to gain independence for

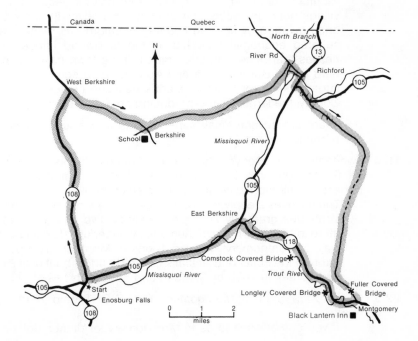

Ireland, marshalled an attack on Canada in 1870. Nearly a thousand Fenians came to Vermont by train from Boston. They fought one small battle—the only violent encounter of their unsuccessful attempt to acquire land for a New Ireland—and then fled back across the border, where the U.S. Marshal promptly arrested their leaders.

8.6 At the crossroad by the Berkshire Elementary School (on the right), turn LEFT onto the unsigned road.

For about a mile you must climb a moderate grade, but then the road turns downward into a wonderful four-mile descent facing one of the most panoramic views in Vermont. Directly before you stands the Jay Peak range; to your left in Canada the hump of Pinnacle Mountain rises above the hills; and on the clearest of days Mount Mansfield is visible far to the south, over your right shoulder.

13.7 At the T, turn RIGHT onto River Road. (There may not be a street sign at this intersection, but you immediately cross a bridge, and in a quarter-mile you pass an Arco station on your right.)

14.3 At the blinker in Richford, turn RIGHT, cross the bridge over the Missisquoi River, and follow the signs onto Route 105 East.

Richford stands in the midst of great natural beauty, but the village bears the scars of misfortune and adversity. More than once ravaged by fire and flooding, Richford has recently also suffered economic hardship as the hardwood lumber businesses that once supported much of the town have fallen on hard times. But in March and April the area comes alive with sugarmaking, for Richford stands near the center of Franklin County, the largest syrup-producing area in Vermont.

There are several small supermarkets and a luncheonette in Richford.

15.0 Two-tenths mile after you cross a set of railroad tracks, turn RIGHT off Route 105 onto the unsigned road. (You immediately pass beneath a railroad trestle and go up a steep hill.)

The hill rises steeply for about three-quarters of a mile and then continues gradually and relentlessly for two and a half miles more to the top. The road then goes wonderfully downhill all the way to Montgomery! At the outskirts of Montgomery it passes through the Fuller or Blackfalls covered bridge, built over Black Falls Creek in 1890 by Sheldon and Savannah Jewett.

22.2 At the Stop Sign in Montgomery, turn RIGHT onto Route 118 North.

If you can arrange to be in Montgomery for dinner, don't miss the Black Lantern Inn. Chef Rita Kalsmith and her raconteur husband Allan, who is also a lawyer, host a delightful inn with superb continental food.

On your right before you leave the village is the Montgomery Village Store, the last place you can buy food until you reach Enosburg Falls.

Off the southwestern side of Route 118—to the left as you ride toward East Berkshire—are two more covered bridges, also built by the Jewetts. Both stretch eighty feet across the Trout River and shade good swimming and fishing holes. You reach the first, known as Longley or Harnois bridge, a mile and a half from Montgomery; it went into use in 1863. The second, the Comstock bridge, was erected twenty years later and is visible two miles after the first.

The downhill run from Berkshire to Richford with Jay Peak at the horizon.

27.1 At the Stop Sign in East Berkshire, turn LEFT onto Route 105 West.

Route 105 has considerably more traffic than any other road on this tour and crosses railroad tracks several times.

33.0 You are back in Enosburg Falls with the green on your left.

Bicycle Repair Services
Endurance Sports, 82 North Main Street, St. Albans, VT (802-524-4685)
Jason's Sport, 108 Lake Street, St. Albans, VT (802-524-3312)

22

Stowe–Morrisville

Easy–to–moderate terrain; 21 miles

Following delightfully untrafficked roads north of Stowe, this tour affords magnificent views of Mount Mansfield and the peaks that surround it. By heading directly into the countryside, you neatly avoid Stowe's tourist accommodations and cycle through an arcadia of small farms and fishing ponds. Nevertheless, because the tour is short, you also have time to visit the "Ski Capital of the East." In fact Stowe is also a warm weather sports center, offering tennis, bicycle racing, horseback riding, rock climbing, hiking swimming, fishing, and golfing on the highest course in the state. There is a competitive edge to the place; year-round most residents of Stowe seem to be working out, sharpening a technique, or mastering some new sport. But despite all this activity and attractions such as the Green Mountain Guild summer theater, Stowe, more than any other skiing center in the state, retains its integrity as a Vermont village: unhurried, independent, and friendly. The goings-on in the area change constantly, but you can get information at the Stowe Area Association on Main Street. The tour begins at the Stowe Community Church (1863), whose graceful, slim spire soars high above the adjacent buildings.

0.0   From the Stowe Community Church follow Route 100 (Main Street) North.

Since there is little opportunity to buy food along the route, you should probably get something before leaving town. Food for Thought, on the east side of Route 100 about one mile south of the church, purveys an extensive selection of natural foods, which you can buy by weight. It also makes delicious, mostly vegetarian, sandwiches on its own whole-grain breads. Delicatessen fare is available in town at Val's Market opposite the church. Or you can treat yourself to a delicious breakfast at The Gables Inn, a mile and a half out of town on Route 108. Innkeepers Sol and Lynn Baumrind serve homemade specialties from 8 a.m. till noon at tables on their lawn facing Mount Mansfield.

1.6   By the Foxfire Inn (on the right), bear LEFT off Route 100 onto Stagecoach Road. (There may not be a street sign there.)

After a mile and a half of relatively level terrain, Stagecoach Road curves uphill for one and two-tenths miles, then levels off for about three-quarters of a mile, and turns uphill again for a half-mile. Once you reach the top, all the difficult climbing of the tour is behind you, and you immediately begin to reap dividends. From the crest the road runs downhill for over a mile to Morristown.

Along Stagecoach Road you get your first long views of Mount Mansfield, at 4,393′ Vermont's highest peak, and its surrounding mountains—Dewey (el. 3,360′), Spruce Peak (el. 3,320′), Madonna (el. 3,640′), and White Face (el. 3,715′).

7.5 At the Stop Sign beside The Corner Store on the right in Morristown, go STRAIGHT to continue north on Stagecoach Road.
     The road shoots downhill again for over a mile. The last half of the hill is steep, occasionally sandy, and ends abruptly at an intersection, so take it slowly and carefully.

8.8 At the T, turn RIGHT onto the unsigned road.
     Within a half-mile you are cycling along Lamoille Lake on your left.

10.2 At the Yield Sign, turn LEFT onto the unsigned road toward Stowe.

10.3 At the Stop Sign, turn LEFT onto Route 100 North.

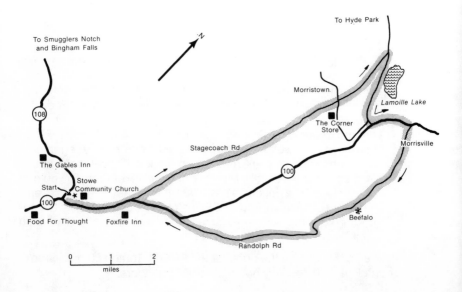

11.0 At the traffic island on the edge of Morrisville, turn RIGHT onto Randolph Road.

In about three miles you reach a pasture on the left where you may see a few wooly red-haired cattle. These rather wild-looking animals are Beefalo, a cross between buffalo and domestic beef cattle.

Soon on your right a sweeping view of the Mount Mansfield range comes into sight. If you use your imagination, you may be able to discern a resemblance between Mansfield and the profile of a human face with forehead, nose, lips, chin, and Adam's apple. After completing your bicycle tour, consider going to the top of Mansfield. You can get there by hiking, driving the toll road, or taking the Mount Mansfield Gondola, which runs on Memorial Day weekend and from mid-June to September. The views from the summit are among the most spectacular in Vermont.

18.6 At the Stop Sign, turn LEFT onto Route 100 South.

21.0 You are back in Stowe by the Community Church.

If the weather is hot and you are feeling like a swim, nothing can rival Bingham Falls, where the West Branch of Little River tumbles through a shaded glen below Smugglers Notch into deep pools of sparkling, cold water. The falls are located about two hundred yards off the east side of Route 108, four and a half miles north of its intersection with Route 100. There is a parking area on the west side of the road across from the path that leads through the woods to the waterfalls.

After you swim, consider continuing north on Route 108 three and a half miles to Smugglers Notch. The Notch, a pass between Mount Mansfield and Sterling Mountain, reaches an elevation of 2,162 feet. It earned its name during the War of 1812 when smugglers took cattle and other commodities through it to Canada in violation of Thomas Jefferson's Embargo Acts. The temperature in the Notch is always markedly lower than elsewhere in the vicinity and sustains rare Ice Age flora not found even at higher elevations. Thousand-foot cliffs rise on either side of the road, and you can frequently see rock climbers clinging to the outcroppings. In the annual June Stowe Bicycle Race cyclists climb through the Notch on the fifty mile course, over which they average nearly twenty-eight miles an hour!

Bicycle Repair Services
Demers Repair, Inc., 81 South Main Street, Barre, VT (802-476-7712)
Onion River Sports, 20 Langdon Street, Montpelier, VT (802-229-9409)
Shaw's General Store, Main Street, Stowe, VT (802-253-4040)

Mount Mansfield as seen from the north.

Northeastern Vermont

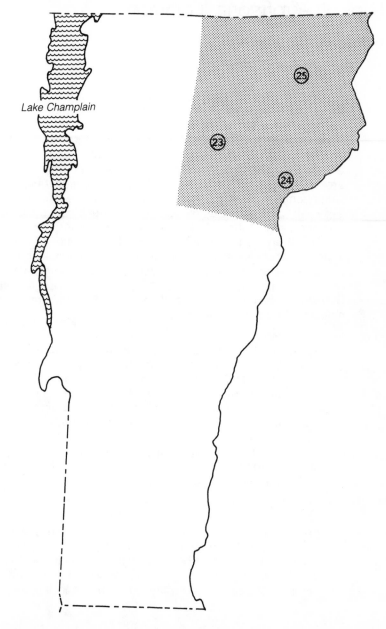

Lake Champlain

23

Wolcott–Craftsbury Common

Difficult terrain; 38 miles

Starting in Wolcott, this tour explores an extraordinary pocket of Vermont's Northeast Kingdom. Named by former U.S. Senator George Aiken, the Northeast Kingdom is roughly a square, forty miles on a side, bordering Canada and New Hampshire. Long an economic backwater, this region of glacial lakes and conifer forests possesses a sort of pastoral magic. The path taken by this tour is no exception, although Craftsbury Common and Greensboro no longer suffer from economic hardship. In that respect the tour highlights an especially privileged part of the Kingdom. But the magic persists: in Caspian Lake, in the nearly deserted road winding its way through the Craftsburys, and in North Wolcott, where lives of hardship in the midst of beauty are still the rule. Spend a full day making the tour, if you can, for few places offer better opportunities to meet such a diversity of people than do Wolcott, Hardwick, Greensboro, and Craftsbury Common. The difficult portion of the tour comes in its first half, and the final third is as easy as it is beautiful.

0.0   Leave Wolcott on Route 15 East toward Hardwick.
Settled in 1789, Wolcott was named after General Oliver W. Wolcott, one of the signers of the Declaration of Independence. You start from this rather drab town in order to complete most of the cycling on Route 15 at the beginning of the tour. As the main thoroughfare across the northern quarter of Vermont, Route 15 draws a substantial amount of traffic, including many trucks. Cycling on this road is usually most pleasant in the morning. Over the six miles from Wolcott to Hardwick you climb very slightly uphill along the Lamoille River, which rises north of Greensboro and flows west into Lake Champlain.

Two miles east of Wolcott on your right, the Fisher covered bridge extends 103 feet over the Lamoille River. Built in 1908 by the St. Johnsbury and Lamoille Railroad Company, it is the last railroad covered bridge in use in Vermont and one of only a few left in the country. A cupola, which runs its full length to provide a vent for the smoke, distinguishes this covered bridge from others. Scheduled for replacement in 1968, the bridge was saved by private donations and state funds, which paid for the installation of supportive steel beams beneath its floor.

5.8   At the T in front of the Hardwick Department Store, turn LEFT to continue on Route 15 East. The next two turns come within a quarter-mile.

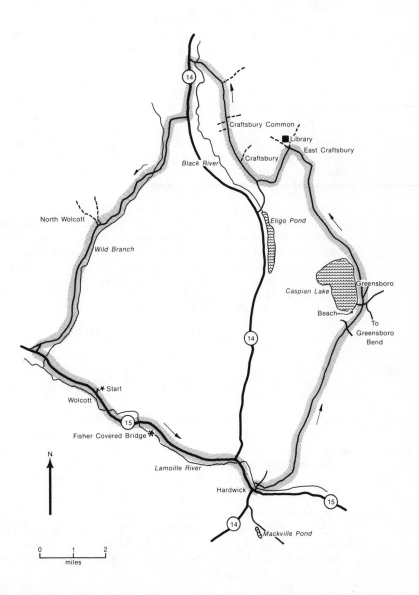

If you feel like swimming, intead of turning left at this T, turn right onto Route 14 South, ride a half-mile, and then turn left toward Mackville. Follow that road three-quarters of a mile to a picnic and swimming area on the right by Mackville Pond.

Hardwick was a simple agricultural town until 1868, when Henry R. Mack discovered granite there. Then the area went through a dramatic transformation, becoming one of the granite centers of the nation. Like a booming mining town, it rode the crest of prosperity into a period of frenetic, haphazard growth. If you are interested in old glass, stop at the Hardwick Pharmacy before you leave town. On display there is a superb collection of apothecary jars more than a century old.

Hardwick has recently gained statewide attention as the home of the Craftsbury Chamber Players. This group of skilled professionals, who teach and perform in metropolitan areas most of the year, gives concerts each Thursday during July and August at 8:30 p.m. They choose to play in the Hardwick Town House because of its exceptional acoustics.

On the last Saturday in July, Hardwick is also home to a major fiddling contest. Drawing performers from throughout New England, this competition also attracts as many as 5,000 spectators. Fiddling contests are great fun, especially if you have the taste and energy for a day of music, revelry, and dancing. The Hardwick event runs from approximately 10:00 a.m. to 7:00 p.m.; admission is charged. To confirm dates and location, contact the Hardwick Police Department (802-472-5475).

You can buy food at several stores in Hardwick or later in Greensboro and Craftsbury.

5.9 Immediately beyond a Gulf station (on the left), turn LEFT off Route 15 onto the unsigned road, which immediately crosses a green iron bridge over the Lamoille River.

6.0 At the crossroad by the large gray stone Memorial Building (on the right), turn RIGHT onto Church Street, though there may not be a street sign there.

The Memorial Building, constructed of local granite, contains a room made of Proctor, Vermont, marble and houses a valuable collection of old coins and paper currency.

This section of the tour is its most strenuous. For the first mile and a half the road rises steadily and steeply. Then after descending for a mile, it rolls over smaller hills for three miles, gaining elevation until it reaches Greensboro at an elevation of 1,463′, 800 feet above Hardwick.

11.8 At the crossroad, go STRAIGHT toward Greensboro.
In three-quarters of a mile you can see on your left a small sign
for a public beach indicating the quarter-mile-long road to
Caspian Lake. Surrounded by low hills and wooded shores,
Caspian ranks as one of Vermont's most beautiful and undis-
turbed large lakes. Its crystalline waters are fed by springs and
offer splendid swimming from a sandy shore at the edge of a
parklike lawn maintained by the town of Greensboro.

12.6 Beside Willey's Store (on the right in Greensboro), bear LEFT toward
East Craftsbury—and away from Greensboro Bend.
Willey's Store offers a fine selection of food for a picnic.
Greensboro has become an expensive, rather exclusive, sum-
mer retreat especially favored by writers and professors.

12.8 At the curve, keep LEFT to follow the main road.
Over the next three miles, the road rolls up and down several short
hills and then goes downhill for four miles into East Craftsbury. At
the crest of the hill it is worth stopping to look at the view of
Caspian Lake.

As you swing through a sharp left curve in East Craftsbury, you
pass the John Woodruff Simpson Memorial Library on the right.
Formerly a community store, this pleasing little building has
been imaginatively transformed. Books and magazines now
line the shelves where groceries and dry goods were once
stacked, and the spacious interior makes a comfortable reading
room.

Just beyond the library, the road bends into an exhilarating two-
mile descent into the Black River Valley.

20.1 At the Stop Sign, turn RIGHT onto the unsigned road that goes
through Craftsbury to Craftsbury Common.
You reach Craftsbury in one mile. If you are not carrying food or
have not already eaten, you should stop at one of the two stores
there, because they are the last ones on the route. Since
Craftsbury Common is much more beautiful and interesting than
Craftsbury, it is worth waiting to picnic there.

Though barely a mile long, the ride up to the broad plateau
where Craftsbury Common sits is demanding. But at the top you
suddenly find yourself in an almost surreal collection of trim
houses, uniformly gleaming with white clapboards and green
shutters, and commanding views across verdant valleys to
mountains in the east and west. Entirely free of commercial
establishments save two craft shops, this airy village surrounding a broad green must be one of the most memorable in

New England. Its spotless neatness accentuates the simplicity of line and color in its architecture. Giant elms and sugar maples shade lawns set behind white picket fences. And elegantly presiding over the village is the towering spire of the United Church of Craftsbury (1820).

During fall foliage season, on the last Saturday of September, the Common's silent dignity gives way to the sounds of country music and slapping hands. The Youth Fellowship and Operation Friendship of the United Church of Craftsbury sponsor a banjo contest. This venerable competition dates to 1967 and attracts 1,500 spectators. The contest starts at noon and runs into the early evening; admission is charged. If you are not interested in banjo music, avoid this tour when the contest is taking place, for it draws extra traffic into the area. To confirm the date and location, contact the United Church of Craftsbury (802-586-2202).

22.3 From Craftsbury Common, continue to follow the main road STRAIGHT through town, keeping the common on your left.

From the Common you glide speedily downhill nearly three miles back into the Black River valley.

Pedaling by the United Church of Craftsbury on Craftsbury Common.

25.0 At the Stop Sign, turn LEFT onto Route 14 South.

27.0 Turn RIGHT off Route 14 onto the unsigned road toward North Wolcott.
You ride gently uphill for a mile and then follow the Wild Branch River until it empties into the Lamoille beside Route 15.

36.0 Bear RIGHT at the fork, go a hundred yards to the Stop Sign, and there turn LEFT onto Route 15 East.

38.0 You reach Wolcott where this tour began.

Bicycle Repair Services
Onion River Sports, 20 Langdon Street, Montpelier, VT (802-229-9409)
Park Pedals, South Walden Road, Cabot, VT (802-563-2252)
Shaw's General Store, Main Street, Stowe, VT (802-253-4040)
St. Jay Hardware, 39 Eastern Avenue, St. Johnsbury, VT (802-748-8076)

24

Barnet–St. Johnsbury

Moderate–to–difficult terrain; 52.5 or 36 miles

From the tiny settlement of Barnet, this tour reaches northward along the Connecticut River uplands, dubbed the Northeast Kingdom by former U.S. Senator George Aiken. The first thirteen miles bring challenge along with beauty as you leave the river valley and ride westward into the hills of Caledonia County. The terrain here is sometimes arduous, but the charm of the Kingdom's tiny towns and undulating hills makes the effort dramatically worthwhile. At its midpoint the tour enters St. Johnsbury and necessitates a little cycling on roads that are neither pretty nor quiet. But that city offers surprising attractions as well: a fine museum of natural history, a remarkable art gallery, superb Victorian architecture, and a comprehensive exhibit of the process of making maple syrup. The tour abandons Vermont for New Hampshire in the final ten miles. There you follow the Connecticut River through pleasing farmlands from which you get rare, long views across the river to Vermont.

0.0 From Pearson's General Store in Barnet, ride west toward West Barnet, Harvey's Lake, and Peacham. Go just fifteen yards and bear LEFT onto Church Street, which is unsigned here. In 150 yards you pass the two-story Barnet Village School on your left.

During the first week of October, Barnet joins Peacham and other nearby towns to sponsor the Northeast Kingdom Annual Fall Foliage Festival. The celebration lasts a week, and a different event is scheduled in each town daily. For information call the Barnet Town Clerk (802-633-2256).

0.3 At the Stop Sign, turn RIGHT toward West Barnet, Harvey's Lake, and Peacham. Thereafter, do not turn onto the side roads.

In a mile and a quarter, you pass Karme-Choling, a Tibetan Buddhist meditation center, which occupies a large red barn and white farmhouse on 430 acres to your right. Guests are welcome just to visit or to stay overnight.

After a relatively easy three miles, you encounter the most difficult part of the tour. For four and a half miles, rolling hill follows rolling hill, as you climb from the Connecticut River to the uplands of Peacham. From an elevation of 452' at Barnet you ascend to 1,000' at South Peacham and then, in barely a mile, 900' more to Peacham (el. 1,908').

4.6   Beside the Lakeview Grange on the right in West Barnet, bear LEFT so you pass the Presbyterian Church of West Barnet on your left and then the West Barnet General Store on your right. This road is called Main Street, but it is unsigned here.

4.9   Just beyond the West Barnet Garage with Mobil gas pumps on the left in West Barnet, turn RIGHT toward Peacham.

6.4   At the T, in front of the South Peacham Store, turn RIGHT toward Danville.

Don't feel weak if you have to stop on this one. For a mile the grade averages 17%!

7.4   In Peacham continue STRAIGHT past the Peacham Store on your left.

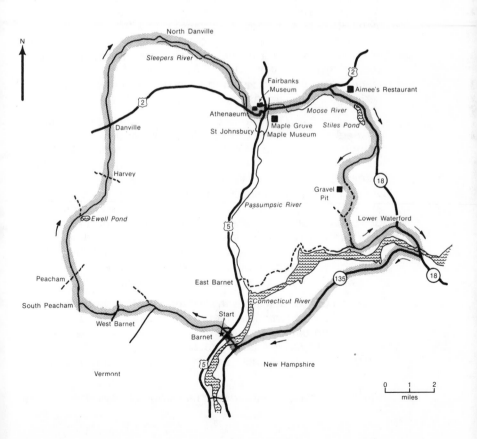

Peacham is a sparkling village of white clapboard houses that date to the eighteenth century. The Peacham Historical Society merits a look if you are intrigued by local history. You can get a key from the Town Clerk or Ed Brown (802-592-3361).

From Peacham to Danville the cycling is much easier. Although the terrain continues its dramatic rolls, you loose nearly 600′ in the next six miles. In the late fall the hillsides are decorated by hundreds of yellow-orange larch trees, also called tamaracks. This unusual genus of pine tree is deciduous; its green needles change color and fall off in the autumn.

14.3 At the blinker in Danville, go STRAIGHT across US 2 onto the road to North Danville.

Danville sits on a plateau, commanding long views of New Hampshire's White Mountains. Thaddeus Stevens was born here in 1792. A vigorous and outspoken opponent of slavery, he also fought Lincoln's plan for reconstructing the south after the Civil War because he considered it too lenient. Leader of the Congressional Radical Republicans, Stevens broke with Andrew Johnson when the latter vetoed a bill to protect the newly freed blacks from vengeful codes being legislated against them by many southern states. Stevens went on to lead the successful battle for the Fourteenth Amendment and to conduct the House impeachment proceedings against Johnson.

In some circles Danville is best known as the dowsing headquarters of the nation. Dowsers locate water and other underground objects by moving a forked stick over the ground until the stick bends downward to indicate a find. For over eighty years members of the American Society of Dowsers have been convening here for a weekend in September to swap stories and trade secrets. On the Sunday morning of that weekend a crowd of dowsers and onlookers always gathers on the green as everyone who wants to try dowsing is given a chance. A good dowser can unsettle the crustiest skeptic. You can obtain further information about dowsing and the Society by writing to the Secretary, American Society of Dowsers, Inc., Danville, VT 05828.

You can buy food at the Danville General Store across from the green; the next ten miles offer many pleasant places to picnic. Or you can eat at the gracious little Creamery Restaurant, on the right, fifty yards after you cross US 2. The Creamery is open seven days a week and features homemade soups and salads.

After climbing gradually for two miles, you glide downhill nearly

seven miles to St. Johnsbury, which lies at an elevation of 655',
more than 700' lower than Danville. The first two miles are
especially fast, and the road may be bumpy and broken.

24.2 At the Traffic Light, go STRAIGHT onto US 2 East toward St.
Johnsbury.

24.8 At the triangle in front of Carl Ranger and Colby Halls of St.
Johnsbury Academy, bear LEFT onto US 2 East and follow it through
St. Johnsbury. If you want to reduce the tour to thirty-six miles, take
US 5 South from St. Johnsbury eleven miles to Barnet. US 5 follows
the Passumpsic River and makes easy riding. Much of the traffic that
formerly used US 5 now takes Interstate 91.

St. Johnsbury Academy, founded in 1842, is a private, coeducational college preparatory boarding school for 650 students.

Situated at the confluence of the Passumpsic, Moose, and
Sleepers rivers, St. Johnsbury with a population of 8,000 is the
largest town in the Northeast Kingdom. Much of its history and
marvelous architecture derives from the imagination and generosity of Thaddeus Fairbanks (1796–1886), inventor of the lever
scale and founder of the Fairbanks–Morse Scale Works. Many
of the grand homes and public buildings along Main Street (US
2) were built between 1830 and 1870, when the company's
prosperity led to the tripling of the city's population.

Three things in St. Johnsbury are particularly interesting. The
Fairbanks Museum of Natural Science (1891) at 83 Main Street
is the city's most elegant architectural work. Lambert Packard
designed it in the Richardsonian style with a facade of red
sandstone and a finely crafted interior featuring an arched oak
ceiling and spiral staircases. The museum contains a comprehensive display of Vermont flora, one of the world's largest
collections of hummingbirds, and an eclectic assortment of other
objects. Adults and children alike can spend hours marveling at
mounted animals from throughout the world, a mummy case, a
suit of armor, old china, pewter, fossils, minerals, and much more.
In the basement physical phenomena are cleverly presented by
push-button displays that almost ask to be manipulated. Outside,
live owls, hawks, reptiles, and small animals are exhibited in
natural habitats. During the summer the museum also sponsors
nature walks to see birds, wildflowers, and places of geological
significance. The museum is open without charge Monday
through Saturday from 10:00 a.m. to 4:00 p.m. and Sunday from
1:00 p.m. to 5:00 p.m.; its planetarium is open 2:30 p.m. to 5:00
p.m., Saturday and Sunday.

The St. Johnsbury Athenaeum at 30 Main Street was built and given to the city by Horace Fairbanks, Thaddeus's nephew. Designed by John Davis Hatch of New York City, the building is another superlative example of Victorian architecture. The Athenaeum contains a 40,000-volume library and an art gallery lit by skylights in a domed ceiling. The gallery is the oldest American art gallery still preserved exactly as it was when it was built in 1873. It houses a permanent collection of nearly one hundred canvases, half being copies of European masterworks and half originals of the Hudson River School. Included are works by Jasper Cropsey, Asher B. Durand, James and William Hart, and Worthington Whittredge. But the *piece de resistance* remains the ten-by-fifteen-foot "Domes of the Yosemite" by Albert Bierstadt. When it was acquired, *The New York Times* lamented that "it is now doomed to the obscurity of a Vermont town where it will astonish the natives." To that, Fairbanks replied, "The people who live in this obscurity are nevertheless quite capable of appreciating the dignity it lends to this small village." Bierstadt was apparently not upset by the painting's location, for he returned every summer until his death to view it and retouch it. The Athenaeum is open without charge Monday through Saturday, 9:30 a.m. to 5:00 p.m. On Monday and Wednesday, it stays open until 8:00 p.m.

As you leave St. Johnsbury on US 2, you pass the Maple Grove Maple Museum on your right. Here you can tour the world's largest maple sugar candy factory, see a movie showing how maple syrup is made—forty gallons of sap make one gallon of syrup—and visit an exhibit of sugarmaking equipment. If you decide to purchase some candy, examine the label closely to see whether you are getting pure maple sugar or a blend of maple and cane sugars. The museum is open from Memorial Day until late October seven days a week from 9:00 a.m. to 5:00 p.m. Admission is charged.

Most of the next three and a half miles are a compromise. The eastern outskirts of St. Johnsbury along US 2 are congested and not pretty, but they form a necessary link in the route.

28.2 At the blinker in front of Aimee's Restaurant—a pleasant place to eat if the weather is poor—turn RIGHT onto Route 18 South toward Lower Waterford.

The road goes uphill for a mile and then levels off beside Stiles Pond. Traffic on Route 18 can get heavy, but not as heavy as US 2.

31.0 At the signs for Waterford Sand & Gravel and the Waterford School, turn RIGHT off Route 18 onto the unsigned road.

33.9   At the gravel pit, on the right, continue STRAIGHT onto the unpaved road.

You follow unpaved roads for two and six-tenths miles from this turn.

35.5   At the T, turn LEFT and continue on the unpaved road.

36.7   At the Stop Sign, just after the road surface becomes paved again, bear LEFT.

Just before the next turn, you ride through the hillside village of Lower Waterford, several houses date to the eighteenth century. Rabbit Hill Inn is located in Lower Waterford, but its excellent dining room does not serve lunch.

39.2 At the Stop Sign, turn RIGHT onto Route 18 South.

40.8 At the Stop Sign just after crossing the Connecticut River into New Hampshire, turn RIGHT onto New Hampshire Route 135 South toward Monroe.

As you ride south on a ridge above the river, you can see Lower Waterford and Barnet rising out of the trees on the Vermont shore. You also encounter several small hills.

51.2 Turn RIGHT onto Barnet Road toward Barnet, Vermont, and ride across the Connecticut River back into the Green Mountain State.

51.6 At the Stop Sign, turn RIGHT onto US 5 North.

52.5 At the second left-turn for West Barnet, Harvey's Lake, and Peacham, turn LEFT and you are back at Pearson's General Store on the left in Barnet.

Bicycle Repair Services
Demers Repair, Inc., 81 South Main Street, Barre, VT (802-476-7712)
Onion River Sports, 20 Langdon Street, Montpelier, VT (802-229-9409)
Park Pedals, South Walden Road, Cabot, VT (802-563-2252)
St. Jay Hardware, 39 Eastern Avenue, St. Johnsbury, VT (802-748-8076)
Village Sports Shop, US 5, Lyndonville, VT (802-626-8448)
Western Auto Associates Store, 34 Depot Street, Lyndonville, VT (802-626-5035)

25

Lakes of the Northeast Kingdom:
A three-day tour

The distance and terrain are stated at the beginning of each day's directions.

Vermont's northern Piedmont and glaciated Connecticut River highlands have been known as the Northeast Kingdom since former U.S. Senator George Aiken so dubbed them in 1949. This region, the most sparsely settled of the state, retains an ethereal quality, difficult to define, yet evident to those who take the time to explore it. This tour, beginning in East Burke, is designed to give you that opportunity.

Totaling as much as 155 miles over three days, the tour seeks out the deep glacial lakes, conifer forests, tiny villages, and hillside farms that evoke the magnificent serenity for which the Kingdom is famous. Each day brings you to a sparkling lake—Island Pond, Lake Willoughby, Crystal Lake, and Lake Seymour—where swimming is a joy. On clear days from the hill towns of Sutton, Sheffield, and Holland you can view the White Mountains of New Hampshire as well as the Green Mountains of Vermont. Indeed, before leaving East Burke drive the toll road up Burke Mountain (el. 3,267'); frost heaves have buckled the road so badly it is not safe to descend by bicycle. At the top nothing obstructs your view, and with the aid of a map you can identify the major geological formations you will soon be seeing by bicycle. The towns along the route offer less of architectural or historical interest than do those in the more prosperous sections of the state. But for me the Northeast Kingdom—in temperament and appearance—is really the Vermonters' Vermont. And the roads are virtually free of traffic.

The tour is deliberately constructed to provide several choices. Actually it is four tours: the first, a circular day trip between East Burke and Barton, described as Day One; the second a circular two-day tour between East Burke and Derby Line, consisting of Days Two and Three; the third, a three-day figure eight combining Days One, Two, and Three in that order; and the fourth, a Century, covering Days Two and Three in twelve hours. The tour is also designed so you may use either country inns or campgrounds and so you encounter the

most difficult rides when you can be free of your panniers.

Do not start this tour until you have contacted the places where you will sleep, for you cannot rely on their being prepared for you without notice. Unless you live nearby, you will surely find it convenient to stay in East Burke the night before you start bicycling.

On the night before you begin cycling and the night between Days One and Two, stay at either the Old Cutter Inn (802-626-5152) or Darling State Park (no telephone). The mailing address for both is simply East Burke, VT 05832. The Old Cutter Inn provides attractive rooms with shared baths in its main building and with private baths in the Carriage House. My favorite rooms are #1, which has two double beds, cheerful, flowered wallpaper, lots of afternoon sunshine, and a bath down the hall, and #7, which faces Mounts Hor and Pisgah, and has two twin beds, its own bathroom, and an outdoor deck. Innkeepers Fritz and Marti Walther serve breakfast as well as fine continental dinners. The inn has a full liquor license, small bar, wood-beamed dining room, and splendid mountain view. Reservations are essential.

Darling State Park in East Burke opens the Friday preceding Memorial Day and closes in mid-October. The park provides twenty-seven tent sites and ten-by-thirteen foot, three-sided, wooden floor lean-tos, hot showers, toilets, water, firewood, ice, and a small store. Vermont state parks do not accept reservations for less than three nights; space is distributed on a first-come, first-served basis.

On the night between Days Two and Three, you can stay at either Char-Bo Campground near Derby or Seymour Lake Lodge in Morgan Center. Char-bo, a private campground and member of VAPCOO, opens May 15 and closes in early October. Owners Robert and Charlotte Knowles welcome reservations for a single night and may be reached at Char-Bo Campground, Box 54, Derby, VT 05829 (802-766-8807). Char-Bo offers swimming in Lake Salem, forty-two campsites, toilets, hot showers, and laundry facilities.

Seymour Lake Lodge is homey, friendly, and rustic. Dan and Gayle Phillabaum and their two children provide a hearty welcome and gladly share their home with guests. The lodge is decorated with hunting and fishing trophies and has a wonderful porch that looks westward to the sunsets over Seymour Lake. Seymour Lake Lodge serves meals but does not have a liquor license; its eight rooms share two and a half baths. Make reservations by contacting Seymour Lake Lodge, Morgan Center, VT 05854 (802-895-2752).

Day One

East Burke–Barton–East Burke: Moderate–to–difficult terrain; 50 miles

0.0   From either the Old Cutter Inn or Darling State Park, follow the Burke Mountain Recreation Area road downhill to East Burke.

2.2   At the Stop Sign in East Burke, turn LEFT onto Route 114 South.
In a hundred yards you pass a grocery on the right and a general store on the left. The classic general store contains the East Burke post office and sells food, hardware, and dry goods. Get your snacks either here in East Burke or in five miles at Lyndonville, for afterwards little is available until you reach Barton.

East Burke's Old School Museum stands three hundred yards south of the general store on the same side of the road. This brown, weathered eighteen-by-twenty-three foot retired schoolhouse contains a potpourri of items from its past: primers, pupils' desks, musical instruments, and a globe made around 1800 by a local resident. The building is neither electrified nor heated and opens only during daylight hours on mild days from June to October. If the door is locked, you can get a key from the caretaker who lives in the white house next door.

7.4   At the blinker on the outskirts of Lyndonville, go STRAIGHT onto US 5 South.

8.0   At the next blinker, which is in Lyndonville, go STRAIGHT off US 5 onto the unsigned road.
If you have not yet gotten food, stop at White Market, on your left at this light.

The Cobleigh Public Library in Lyndonville contains an interesting collection of Vermontiana, old coins, stuffed New England birds, and an eighteenth-century grandfather's clock. The library is open Monday through Saturday from 1:30 p.m. to 5:00 p.m. On Wednesday evenings during the summer, the Lyndonville band performs at the bandstand in Powers Park across from White Market. The Caledonia Country Fair, which in true Vermont style combines livestock and agricultural exhibitions with the attractions of a traveling carnival, also happens at Lyndonville during August. For further information contact the Lyndonville Town Clerk, 24 Main Street, Lyndonville, Vt 05851 (802-626-5785).

8.2   At the Stop Sign in Lyndonville, turn RIGHT onto Center Street and follow the signs for Route 122 North.

You pass Lyndon Institute, a coeducational boarding secondary school, on your left, go through Miller's Run covered bridge (1878), and then bear left onto Route 122—all within three-quarters of a mile.

A mile and a half beyond Wheelock, Route 122 begins working its way uphill through Sheffield for three and a half miles. The grade begins gently but turns steep in the final mile. The top of the hill marks the Connecticut River–Lake Champlain watershed; most rivers to the east flow into the former, while those to the west flow into the latter. Pause to look behind you at the view; on clear days you can see all the way to New Hampshire's Mount Washington. Then enjoy the three-and-a-half-mile downhill run that lies ahead.

In 1785, during Vermont's brief tenure as an independent nation (1777–91), the General Assembly took the unusual action of granting land to a college in another country. Having no college of its own and wishing to insure its sons' opportunities for learning, Vermont granted half the township of Wheelock to New Hampshire's Dartmouth College. As late as 1815 the rentals Wheelock townspeople paid to Dartmouth accounted for a major portion of the college's revenues. Wheelock still pays a small annual sum to Dartmouth. In return the college charges no tuition to those sons and, more recently, daughters of Wheelock who qualify for admission.

About two miles down the hill on Route 122 you pass on your right the home of the Bread and Puppet Theater. It is across the road from a garage with a multi-colored, brightly painted roof. This innovative company, which has toured widely in the United States and abroad, uses gigantic masks, hand puppets, and mime in forceful and fun-loving, often political, dramatizations, frequently performed outdoors. Guests are welcome to stop and see the company's marvelous puppets, which present a striking scene in the enormous barn. It is very much worth visiting.

23.0 At the Stop Sign, turn RIGHT onto Route 16 North.

In three miles you pass the Barton Fairgrounds on your left. Some of the major shows exhibited there are the Memorial Day Horse Show, the Arts and Crafts Show in early August, and the Orleans County Fair in mid-August. For more information contact the Chamber of Commerce, Barton, VT 05822.

27.0 At the intersection in Barton, turn RIGHT onto US 5 South.

Since no stores fall along the next fifteen miles of your path, make certain you have what you want before leaving. If you carry your lunch along, you can picnic within a few miles on the shore of Crystal Lake.

34.0 One-quarter mile beyond a small lumber mill and Bean Pond on your left, bear RIGHT off US 5 onto the road to Sutton. (Look carefully for this turn; it is easy to miss.)

As soon as you turn you pass beneath a railroad trestle and begin to climb a formidable hill. About six-tenths of a mile up you can refill your water bottle at a mountain spring on the right. The grade of the hill tapers off a short way past the spring and remains gradual for another two miles. On the top you cycle for roughly a mile along a plateau, from which the views eastward are superb. Then you glide downhill into Sutton.

39.0 At the tiny grass traffic island just beyond the Sutton Elementary School—partially obscured by foliage on your right—turn LEFT toward West Burke. (Try to approach this turn slowly, for it too is easy to miss.)

The road from Sutton goes downhill for a half-mile, up for three-quarters, and down the rest of the way to West Burke. It offers exceptional views of Burke Mountain to your right, but keep your eye on the road during the final descent, for it is fast, and suddenly curves ninety degrees to the left.

41.8 After crossing the railroad tracks, bear LEFT onto the unsigned road.

42.0 At the Stop Sign in West Burke, turn RIGHT onto US 5 South, go just past the K & G Market (on the left), and then turn LEFT onto Route 5A North. In fifty yards, as soon as you cross a bridge, turn RIGHT off Route 5A onto the road toward Burke Hollow and East Burke. (All these turns occur within a quarter-mile; all roads you take are paved.)

The ride from West Burke through Burke Hollow can be arduous after all the cycling you have done. You must climb a gradual three-quarter-mile-long hill in the first two miles and then a very steep one of the same length just beyond Burke Hollow. The second climb ends by a cemetery and gives way to an easy, occasionally downhill, ride into East Burke.

The Union Meeting House, which sends its delicate spire high above the rooftops of Burke Hollow, remains unaltered, save fresh white paint, since its construction in 1825. It is worth stopping—either now or tomorrow when you come by again—to see the old box pews, each with its own door, and the high barrel pulpit.

47.1 At the Yield Sign on the edge of East Burke, turn LEFT onto the unsigned road and ride a tenth of a mile across the bridge.

47.2   At the Stop Sign in East Burke, turn LEFT onto Route 114 North.

47.5   At the sign for Burke Mountain Recreation Area, turn RIGHT onto the road to the Old Cutter Inn and Darling State Park.
As you may recall, this hill is unrelenting, but the grade is moderate to gentle most of the way.

50.0   You are back at your starting point.

Day Two

East Burke to Seymour Lake Lodge: moderate terrain; 51 miles
East Burke to Char-Bo Campground direct: easy–to–moderate terrain; 31 miles
East Burke to Char-Bo Campground via Morgan Center: moderate terrain; 60 miles

0.0   From either the Old Cutter Inn or Darling State Park, follow the Burke Mountain Recreation Area road downhill to East Burke.
Before you start bicycling, find a vantage point with an unobstructed view to the north. There, slightly to the west of north, you can see the prominent, hummocklike peaks of Mounts Hor and Pisgah. They define the glacial canyon within which lies Lake Willoughby and through which you will soon be riding.

2.2   At the Stop Sign in East Burke, turn LEFT onto Route 114 South.
Buy some food for snacks and a picnic lunch at one of the stores in East Burke or later on in Westmore. If you are planning to take the thirty-one-mile route to Char-Bo Campground, buy your dinner too.

2.5   Turn RIGHT toward Burke Hollow and West Burke. Go across the bridge and then turn RIGHT toward Burke Hollow.
You are leaving East Burke by the roads you returned on yesterday. For the first mile and a half you climb a gentle grade. Then, from the cemetery on your right, you descend quickly three-quarters of a mile into Burke Hollow.

5.4   Just beyond the Union Meeting House (on the right) in Burke Hollow, bear LEFT and then immediately bear RIGHT to follow the main road to West Burke.
Yesterday's climb is now a descent which makes the two miles to West Burke an easy ride.

7.6   At the Stop Sign in West Burke, turn RIGHT onto Route 5A North.
If you still need food or supplies, turn left at this Stop Sign and

ride a tenth of a mile to the two stores in West Burke. Route 5A stays relatively flat until it passes the northern end of Lake Willoughby, when it goes up a moderately steep hill for a mile.

Set directly between the rocky faces of Mounts Hor (el. 2,751') and Pisgah (el. 2,646'), Lake Willoughby measures six miles from north to south and 600' deep. Its strikingly clear waters make excellent swimming as well as fishing and can be reached most easily from beaches at its northern and southern ends. The largest fish known to be caught in Vermont waters came from Lake Willoughby. A forty-six-inch lake trout with a girth of twenty-five inches, it weighed thirty-four pounds.

By a quirk of nature, rare, delicate Arctic plants grow on the cliffs of Mount Pisgah. Mostly calcicoles, which take the calcium they need from the rocks they cling to, these relics of the Ice Age find the moist, protected ledges of Pisgah hospitable. A hiking trail leads to the summit of Mount Pisgah from the east side of Route 5A, a half-mile south of the southern tip of Lake Willoughby. About seven miles round-trip, the hike is moderately difficult and takes approximately four and a half hours.

27.0 At the Stop Sign outside West Charleston, turn LEFT onto Routes 5A North and 105 West.
    Irving Dane's General Store in West Charleston—on your left in a mile—is the last place to shop on the thirty-one-mile route to Char-Bo Campground. The area between West Charleston and Derby was a favorite hunting ground of the St. Françis Indians. Routes 5A and 105 follow a gently rolling course.

31.0 The entrance to Char-Bo Campground a quarter-mile off the road is on your right.
    If you are taking the sixty-mile route, you might want to stop at the campground to unburden yourself of your heavier gear. But remember to take along some packing equipment if you intend to pick up supplies before your return. The next twenty-nine miles pose a greater challenge than the first thirty-one.

33.5 At the intersection in Derby Center, go STRAIGHT onto US 5 North.

34.7 By the Shamrock Shop, a wooden building with a small attached greenhouse (on the right), turn LEFT off US 5 onto the road toward Beebe Plain.

37.2 At the first intersection with a paved road, turn RIGHT onto the unsigned road.
    Immediately after turning, you must climb a steep hill three-quarters of a mile long.

The shoreline road along Lake Willoughby with Mount Hor in the background.

39.0 At the Stop Sign beside St. Edward's Church on the outskirts of Derby Line, turn LEFT onto US 5 North.

39.5 At the blinker in Derby Line, turn RIGHT toward Interstate 91.
        If you would like to cross the border into Canada, this is the most convenient place to do so. Take along some identification in case U.S. Customs requests it when you return and simply go straight from this blinker a hundred yards into Quebec. The Opera House and Haskell Free Library in Derby Line exemplify the casual view often taken of the international border in this part of the country. The books in the library and the stage of the Opera House lie in one country while the checkout desk and the audience remain in the other.

        If Seymour Lake Lodge is your destination and you would like a drink when you arrive, buy your beer or wine in Derby Line. Also be sure you have all the food you want for the final eleven and a half miles, for not a single store sits along your route between Derby Line and Morgan Center, and the ride is not easy. From Derby Line to the crossroad that marks Holland, you climb 400' in elevation along roads that roll more up than down over moderately steep, short hills.

46.0 At the intersection one-half mile beyond the Holland Elementary School (on the left), turn RIGHT onto the unsigned road.
        The balance of the ride to Morgan Center goes mostly downhill and near the end provides a lovely long view of Seymour Lake.

51.0 At the Stop Sign in Morgan Center, you are facing Seymour Lake. Immediately to your left is the Seymour Lake Lodge where you end the day's ride unless you are camping. If you are following the sixty-mile route to Char-Bo Campground, turn RIGHT at this Stop Sign onto Route 111 West.
        Route 111 looks in contour like the teeth of a rip-saw. For four miles the road rolls relentlessly up and down short, steep hills.

55.0 At the second intersection with a paved road on the left, which comes two miles beyond The Morgan Store (on the left), turn LEFT onto the unsigned road.
        The Morgan Store stocks an excellent supply of fresh meats and groceries, some produce, beer, and wine—plenty to fill your panniers for dinner and breakfast at the campground. In a half-mile, the road to West Charleston becomes unpaved for a half-mile, but the surface is smooth and firm and, like the rest of this road, slopes gently downward.

57.0 At the Stop Sign in West Charleston, turn RIGHT onto Route 5A

North and 105 West.

60.0 The entrance to Char-Bo Campground leads off Route 105 to your right.

Day Three

Seymour Lake Lodge to East Burke: moderate terrain; 54.6 or 44.6 miles

Char-Bo Campground to East Burke: easy–to–moderate terrain; 42.6 or 32.6 miles

0.0 From Seymour Lake Lodge, turn RIGHT onto Route 111 West.
Over the first four miles Route 111 rolls over short, steep hills shaped like the teeth of a rip-saw. The last five miles, leading into Derby Center, also roll, but less frequently and more gently. You can buy something to carry along for a snack at The Morgan Store, two miles from Seymour Lake Lodge on the left side of Route 111.

9.0 At the Stop Sign in Derby Center, turn LEFT onto Routes 5A South and 105 East.
The next seven miles follow roads you cycled yesterday in the opposite direction.

12.0 From Char-Bo Campground, turn LEFT onto Routes 5A South and
(0.0) 105 East.
For the next four miles you cycle along roads that yesterday you rode in the opposite direction.

16.0 At the fork one mile south of West Charleston, bear LEFT onto Route
(4.0) 105 East toward Island Pond.
In a mile and a half you ride up a gradual mile-long hill and then descend for the same distance. Another mile and a half brings you to East Charleston, where you can select snacks or food for a picnic at the East Charleston Store, on the right.

26.0 At the intersection of Routes 105 and 114, bear LEFT onto Routes
(14.0) 105 East and 114 North toward Island Pond.
If you would like to shorten your tour by ten miles—and skip the ride which circles Island Pond—do not go straight at this intersection. Instead, turn right onto Route 114 South and continue according to the directions below from mileage 35.8 (23.8). If you take the short cut be sure that you have all the food and drink you want; nothing is available on Route 114.

28.0 At the Stop Sign in Island Pond, which is the name of both the town
(16.0) and the lake, turn RIGHT onto Route 105 East.

Before leaving town, be certain you have all the food you want for the balance of the day, for there is nowhere to shop again until you reach East Burke.

30.0 Turn RIGHT off Route 105 onto the road toward Brighton State **(18.0)** Park.

31.0 The lawn at Brighton State Park stretches one hundred fifty yards **(19.0)** from the right side of the road to the beach on Island Pond.
The park supplies changing rooms, toilets, picnic tables, and a lifeguard; admission is charged. Island Pond takes its name from the twenty-two acre island in its center. The swimming is excellent, and the park makes a delightful picnic spot. After stopping, continue bicycling in the direction you were headed.

33.0 At the Stop Sign, turn LEFT onto Routes 114 South and 105 **(21.0)** West.

35.8 At the intersection, turn LEFT to continue on Route 114 South toward **(23.8)** Burke Mountain and Lyndonville.
If you are looking for a picnic spot, try the lawn by the Methodist Church on the right in East Haven, nine miles south of this intersection. The first two and a half miles of Route 114 climb steadily to the top of a hill which then gives way to a gentle three-mile descent. From there through East Haven to East Burke, the terrain remains flat, and the cycling is easy unless a headwind strikes you.

52.4 At the sign for Burke Mountain Recreation Area (on the left) just **(40.4)** outside the village of East Burke, turn LEFT onto the road to the Old Cutter Inn and Darling State Park.

54.6 You are back where you began your tour, and now as you look out **(42.6)** toward Willoughby Gap perhaps you understand a little of the mystery of Vermont's Northeast Kingdom.

Bicycle Repair Services
Great Outdoors Trading Company, 73 Main Street, Newport, VT (802-334-2831)
Motion Sports, Route 105, Newport Center, VT (802-334-7029)
Onion River Sports, 20 Langdon Street, Montpelier, VT (802-229-9409)
Park Pedals, South Walden Road, Cabot, VT (802-563-2252)
Village Sports Shop, US 5, Lyndonville, VT (802-626-8448)
Western Auto Associates Store, 34 Depot Street, Lyndonville, VT (802-626-5035)

Appendix

ORGANIZATIONS
Bicycle USA (formerly League of American Wheelmen)
Box 988
Baltimore, MD 21203 (301-727-2022)

Bicycle USA is the oldest member-supported organization serving the interests of bicyclists and representing them before public regulatory and legislative bodies. It disseminates information about the activities and upcoming events of more than 400 affiliated bicycle clubs and lists homes which extend free lodging to touring members. Members also receive an informative monthly magazine.

Bikecentennial: The Bicycle Travel Association
Box 8308
Missoula, MT 59807 (406-721-1776)

Bikecentennial is a member-supported bicyclists' resource center. It offers the nation's most extensive inventory of touring information, books, and maps as well as a remarkable insurance program whereby members can obtain coverage for their bicycles. Since developing the TransAmerica Trail to celebrate the bicentennial of the American Revolution, Bikecentennial has continued to develop a network of long cycling routes.

United States Cycling Federation
1750 East Boulder
Colorado Springs, CO 80909 (303-578-4573)

The USCF is the governing and licensing authority of amateur bicycle racing in the U.S. It is also responsible for Olympic development and depends on private support.

Vermont Bicycle Touring
Box 711-JB
Bristol, VT 05443 (802-453-4811)

Founded by the author in 1972, VBT is the originator of country inn bicycling vacations in America. Tours are open to cyclists of all ages and range in difficulty from very easy to challenging. VBT offers weekend and 5-day van-supported tours that can be linked into vacations of up to thirty days. VBT also runs a Bicycle Tour Planning Service for independent cyclists and a Bicycle Repair Clinic.

Vermont Massage Guild
P.O. Box 124
Ripton, VT 05766 (802-388-2546)

Formed in 1979, the Guild is an organization of professional massage prac-
tioners. In its own words, "Massage is a healing art, the aim of which is to
soothe and relax you. Our members approach this through a variety of
techniques." One reason bicycle racers shave their legs is to facilitate
massage, which is a regular part of their regimen. It's good medicine for
touring cyclists too, for it helps dispel lactic acid, a principal source of the
muscle soreness that often follows strenous exercise. The Guild will send you
a free statewide listing of its members.

PERIODICALS
Bicycle Sport
P.O. Box 5277
Torrance, CA 90510

This monthly magazine began publication in 1983 with articles about
physical fitness, touring bicycles, mountain bikes, and other products of
interest to bicyclists.

Bicycling Magazine
33 E. Minor Street
Emmaus, PA 18049 (215-967-5171)

Bicycling is America's most widely circulated cycling magazine. Published
nine times a year, it normally includes well over a hundred pages of
advertisements and articles about touring, racing, equipment, conditioning,
medical topics, and technical problems.

Velo-News
Box 1257
Brattleboro, VT 05031 (802-254-2305)

Printed in tabloid newspaper form, *Velo-News* is America's most authoritative
racing publication. Not only does it make interesting reading; many of its
stories—especially those on technical subjects like choosing a bicycle of the
proper size and design—give insightful advice to touring cyclists as well.

Winning: Bicycle Racing Illustrated
1524 Linden Street
Allentown, PA 18102 (215-821-6862)

The godchild of two of America's foremost racers, Dave Chauner and Jack
Simes, *Winning* began publication in 1983 and focuses its glossy monthly
pages on the international racing scene and its major personalities. It makes
exciting reading and will urge any cyclist back onto his/her bicycle.

BOOKS

Anybody's Bike Book by Tom Cuthbertson (Ten Speed Press, Berkeley, CA; 1971) is a cleverly written, reliable, and well-illustrated informal guide to bicycle repair.

Bike Touring: The Sierra Club Guide to Outings on Two Wheels by Raymond Bridge (Sierra Club Books, San Francisco, CA; 1979) is a general and comprehensive guide to bicycle touring. Its 450 pages discuss riding techniques, bicycles, wheels, brakes, clothing, camping and carrying gear, and other matters—most dealing with *materiel*—of concern to bicycle tourists. The book is illustrated and well-indexed.

DeLong's Guide to Bicycles & Bicycling by Fred DeLong, (Chilton Book Company, Radnor, PA; 1974) is the encyclopedic work about bicycle hardware and the art of cycling by one of bicycling's technical wizards, who often also contributes to *Bicycling Magazine*. His book is well illustrated and indexed.

The Bicycling Book: Transportation, Recreation, Sport by John Krausz and Vera van der Reis Krausz (The Dial Press, New York, NY; 1982) is a 280-page eclectic collection of articles by an international array of writers. It contains 400 illustrations, ranging from sublime to highly-instructive. The variety of articles, all by highly-regarded persons, is truly ecumenical. This book will be a stimulating and instructive source of entertainment for both newcomers and saddle-hardened tourists. It too has a useful index.

The Bicycle Touring Book: the Complete Guide to Bicycle Recreation by Tim and Glenda Wilhelm (Rodale Press, Emmaus, PA; 1980) is a 300-page comprehensive guide. It is written by a husband/wife team who were among the first to bicycle across the U.S. with two small children. The text is complimented by 150 photographs and illustrations as well as an index.

Guidebooks from Backcountry Publications and The Countryman Press

Written for people of all ages and experience, these highly popular and carefully prepared books feature detailed directions, notes on points of interest, sketch maps, and photographs.

For Bicyclists—

20 Bicycle Tours in New Hampshire, by Tom and Susan Heavey $5.95

20 Bicycle Tours in the Finger Lakes, by Mark Roth and Sally Walters $6.95

25 Bicycle Tours in Eastern Pennsylvania, by Dale Adams and Dale Speicher $6.95

20 Bicycle Tours In and Around New York City, by Dan Carlinsky and David Heim $6.95

About Vermont—

Vermont: An Explorer's Guide, by Christina Tree and Peter S. Jennison $10.95

Fifty Hikes in Vermont, by Ruth and Paul Sadlier $7.95

Canoe Camping Vermont and New Hampshire Rivers, by Roioli Schweiker $4.95

A Year With New England's Birds: Twenty-five Field Trips, by Sandy Mallett $5.95

Other Guides—

Maine: An Explorer's Guide, by Christina Tree $9.95

Fifty Hikes in the White Mountains, by Daniel Doan $8.95

Fifty More Hikes in New Hampshire, by Daniel Doan $8.95

Fifty Hikes in Maine, by John Gibson $8.95

Fifty More Hikes in Maine, by Cloe Catlett $8.95

Fifty Hikes in Connecticut, by Gerry and Sue Hardy $8.95

Fifty Hikes in Central New York, by William Ehling $8.95

Canoeing Central New York, by William Ehling $8.95

Fifty Hikes in the Adirondacks, by Barbara McMartin $8.95

25 Ski Tours in the White Mountains, by Daniel and Sally Ford $5.95

Available from bookstores, sporting goods stores, or the publisher. For a complete description of these and other guides, write The Countryman Press and Backcountry Publications, PO Box 175, Woodstock, VT 05091.